KW-554-793

Copyright Information

PERFECT PAPER
Copyright © 2009 Page One Publishing Pte Ltd

Published and distributed in Europe and Latin America by
INDEX BOOK S.L.
Consell de Cent 160, local 3, 08015 Barcelona
T +34 93 454 5547, F +34 93 454 8438
ib@indexbook.com, www.indexbook.com

First published in 2009 by Page One Publishing Pte. Ltd.
20 Kaki Bukit View, Kaki Bukit Techpark II, Singapore 415956
T +65 6742 2088, F +65 6744 2088
enquiries@pageonegroup.com, www.pageonegroup.com

EDITOR AND AUTHOR
Adeline Loh

ART DIRECTOR
Frédéric Snauwaert

DESIGNER
Feng Dexian

ISBN 978-84-92643-01-1

Typeset in Absara

All rights reserved. No part of this publication may be reproduced, stored in any retrieval system or transmitted, in any form or by any means, electronic, mechanical, photocopying, recording or otherwise, without prior permission in writing from the publisher. For information, contact Page One Publishing Pte Ltd.

Printed and bound by Dami Editorial & Printing Services, Shenzhen, China.

Image Credits

Kako Ueda, pp.10-15
All images courtesy of Kako Ueda and George Adams Gallery, New York

Emma van Leest, pp.22-23
2 *Photography: Daniel Dorall*

Peter Callesen, pp.46-53
All images courtesy Hylene Nyborg Contemporary

Jens Praet, pp.92-95
1 *Photography: Frans van Lieshout.*
3 *Photography: Jens Praet*
4 *Photography: Bas Helders*

PUSH>, pp.112-115
1-4 *Photography: Bettina Meckel*

Maslen & Mehra, pp.136-137
1 *Photography: Sinisa Savic. Images courtesy Maslen & Mehra and Galerie Caprice Horn/Berlin.*

Papering the Body opening, pp.152-153
Photography: Henrik Adamsen

Giovanna Grimoldi, pp.162-163
1 *Photography: David Bailey*
2-3 *Photography: M. Bertari*

Michael Cepress, pp.166-169
1-4 *Photography: Michelle Moore*

Violise Lunn, pp.184-189
1, 3, 4, 6 *Photography: Thomas Petri*
2, 5 *Photography: Henrik Adamsen*

perfect paper

softseating. Brown kraft paper (50% recycled content), 2006. By molo.

Contents

Introduction

There are two things that *Perfect Paper* is not. The first, *Perfect Paper* is unlikely to fit into any conventional historiography of the uses of paper, from the ancient papyrus to the humble toilet paper. The cultural, symbolic and functional uses of paper through time are more fully documented elsewhere. The second, *Perfect Paper* is not a selection of paper works by individuals who identify themselves to be solely paper artists. Rather, *Perfect Paper* is a book of works in paper by today's artists, architects, illustrators, graphic designers, industrial designers, fashion designers and photographers with varying intentions, processes of making and aesthetics styles.

Perfect Paper is an inspiration and idea book. At the heart of the book is the medium, one which has intrigued, enchanted, provoked and gripped enthusiastic creative spirits to learn paper's ways and capabilities. The expressive qualities of paper that emerge are truly contradictory. Some celebrate paper's fragility and lightness to design dresses and objects of ethereal beauty, evoking paper as a medium of unspoken expressiveness where worlds, stories and fantasies are given startling embodiment. Yet others have made accelerated inroads into alternative realms like fashion design and product design, manufacturing paper furniture and vessels that withstand water and weight.

Departing from paper's pervasive use as a printing material, *Perfect Paper* explores the unconventional uses of paper in four chapters. *Illustrative Paper-cuts* showcases two-dimensional paper-cutting works with contemporary imagery; *Arty Objects* explores three-dimensional paper objects and sculptures; *Interiors & Installations* examines paper's potential as a material in tactile furniture and spatial installations; and *Papering the Body* exhibits paper clothing and jewellery that frame the human silhouette. What is revealed is the potential of this ordinary material with unordinary capacities.

The works in *Perfect Paper* can be understood as part of a much larger debate on the separate positions of art, craft and design, and the validity of these distinct positions when one gets involved in the process of making. What can be observed in these paper works is a blurring of the boundaries between art, craft and design, in a generous crossing of impulses, sensibilities and practises that makes the conceptual designer also consummate craftsmen, and the industrial designer preoccupied with concepts typically associated with the fine artist.

Everyday assumptions about paper are thus challenged. Is paper just a fragile and disposable material? What fresh products can it be applied into? Is paper suitable for making both a functional and beautiful object? Can traditional paper crafts have any new relevance in consumer and visual culture? In putting together a book on such a broad spectrum of paper works, there are no overarching theories of what these paper works represent. Nonetheless, the interest in paper and the creative spirit inherent in these works suggest several areas of shifting sands in the larger design climate.

In a broader context, as environmental sustainability becomes more pressing, artists and designers are exploring eco-friendly materials and methods. Paper's recyclable properties are well known and it offers itself as a cheap, easily available and versatile material to create eco-friendly products. The application of paper in various products also reveals a concern with conceptual thinking and the cutting-edge outcomes of independent design practice. A generation of designers, thinking critically and questioning preconceptions, are experimenting with materials to give it fresh applications, allowing us to see a material's potential anew.

In some of these paper works, one can also hear the clarion call of DIY culture: let's get back to making with our hands; let's reject mass production and return to work with a human touch that appeal to our senses and establish their intimacy with the user. The popularity of crafted items, be it at flea markets or on high-street shops and catwalks, suggest possessing an object with the mark of its creator – a crafted object made with care, skill and passion – is gaining relevance in a increasingly technologised environment. Highly-crafted objects by artisans leave us with admiration and awe. The makers of these paper works are concerned with the achievement of craft and human creativity, in which paper offers them a means of expression, whether they identify themselves as artist, independent designer or amateur.

In the hands of today's most progressive artists and designers, paper has undergone an unlikely renaissance. Through deeply satisfying engagements with paper either through the sweat of labour, the slow development of skill, or the exhilaration of material experimentation, the works in *Perfect Paper* give voice to a unique group of visual artists creating the objects and images that surround us.

Perfect Paper does not merely celebrate the possibilities of its medium, paper, itself; it reminds us that the path to creativity is often an individual one, and the heights to which personal passions and values can be given expression. *Perfect Paper* will delight those interested in the bold and beautiful forms captured here. Packed with visually arresting work and artist interviews, *Perfect Paper* is set to enchant collectors and inspire spontaneous creative processes amongst designers.

The Old Man and The Sea. *The Old Man and The Sea* by Ernest Hemingway, 2006. By Holly Ormrod.

Illustrative Paper-cuts

Slowly, by-hand, with a cutting knife.

In the quiet corners of studios around the world, the age-old craft of paper-cutting perseveres. This decorative craft is a unique blend of pictures and the skill of the practiced hand. In paper-cuts, the images tell stories, express an individual's imagination, hint at the maker's cultural and artistic influences; in paper-cutting, we witness the deftness of technique, the individual's love of making, the rare touch of the human hand in a digital age. Practised for millennia in the cultures of China, Japan, Mexico, Israel, Germany and Switzerland, paper-cutting has shed some of its traditional, cultural and religious imagery to assimilate the breadth of images from today's visual culture.

Illustrative Paper-cuts showcases an engaging array of paper-cuts created by an international set of artists and designers. *Illustrative Paper-cuts* reveals how this age-old craft is being infused with images ranging from the whimsical and magical, the intricate and complex, the structured and systematic, to the ghostly and abstract. Much like illustrations, these paper-cut works beg attention for their graphic elements as much as the silent hours of toil and the diversity and qualities of different paper types. *Illustrative Paper-cuts* brings to the fore the wonder that paper-cuts provoke, celebrating the modern face of an ancient craft.

Poisson. 60gsm black paper, 2007. By Aoyama Hina

Kako Ueda

United States & Japan

"I had an open studio a couple of years ago. A middle-aged lady who happened to wonder into my studio was looking at my unfinished piece, *Eros & Thanatos*, and said "You are nuts to do this,"" recalls Japanese paper-cutting artist Kako Ueda who works out of Brooklyn, New York, "What a great compliment."

Ueda has cut her way to around 35 pieces since 2003 with a quiet obsession. The artist, who is often quoted as saying the medium found her, not the other way around, has nonetheless taken her accidental love to another level; "I like its smell and touch. It is such a sensual material," comments Ueda. She indulges a peculiar partiality for organic creatures – insects, animals, plants, human beings – out of fascination with the ways these "natural" beings are constantly being affected and changed by culture. She references art, medical history, world myths, fairly tales, religion (especially Taoism) and philosophy. The ancient Greek idea of the macrocosm and the microcosm continue to find their way into her paper-cuts.

1

1 Self Portrait (Octopus Head). Black *washi* paper, 2007.
2 PJS (Portrait Series I). Hand-cut pH-neutral paper with acrylic, 2006.

2

How did you start working with paper?
I stumbled upon paper cutting in 2003. At that time, I just returned to New York from Japan, taking care of my very sick mother, so I was mentally and physically exhausted. One night, I started playing with any material I could get my hands on – paper, pencil, and scissors. In retrospect, I am glad I didn't start paper-cutting based on some intellectual discourse or reasoning. Whatever state I was psychically in at that time helped me to explore the medium freely. I was so excited on my first attempt, I continued cutting – immediately, I switched from the scissors to an X-Acto knife.

That process of trying out different tools and methods sounds quite intuitive for you. Is it hard to explain that process to someone else? As one critic has written, "craft and theory are water and oil".
Yes, it is true. It is actually so intuitive that it is hard to explain. Some people ask me where I learned the cutting technique. I simply started cutting one day and continued with it. I try to cut according to my own drawings, and sometimes against my drawings to be able to execute the idea for that particular piece better. Any technique, if you can call it that, I seem to have, I must have learned it by just doing it.

You describe your paper-cuts as "something of a hybrid, an object that is both drawing and sculpture".
Well, I am a hybrid myself, being born in Japan but have spent all of my adult life in the States, it makes sense that what I make doesn't fit into one category. In Japan where I am from, the distinction between craft and art is not so clear. A good crafted object needs an artistic sensibility and good art object often requires a high level of execution or craft.

However, people tend to want to define when the lines between art and craft are often blurry.
For convenience and other reasons, humans are experts in categorising. We simply love labelling people and animals etc. There is no doubt that painting and marble sculpture are "art" in the general public's eye, but something made from paper is another story. The more the merrier if my work can fit into two or more worlds.

Your paper-cuts resemble modern illustrations, but the craft itself has a long history and heritage, especially in Japan where you were from.
I started looking into the history of paper-cutting in different cultures. I read about Japanese stencil making for *kimono* wear, various examples of the German *Scherenschnitte*, the Mexican *Papel picado* and Chinese paper-cutting. Every medium has its own history and the public's view on a particular medium varies according to the time and place. In the end, what we call craft or art is in our own head and it truly doesn't matter. A work exists in front of you and if it speaks to you, then it is relevant.

Do people generally find your work accessible?
All of my pieces contain familiar images of organisms and body parts so they are probably quite friendly to many people's eyes. It would be nice if different viewers could somehow relate to my work on different levels. It is up to a viewer to weave his/her own story line using various characters (elements/components) which exist within each piece.

What does it take to be a good contemporary paper-cutting artist?
That is a loaded question. A good paper-cutting artist is a person who has sensibility towards paper as a material. She/he explores the possibilities that paper has at its maximum at the same time expresses her/his own unique view of the world, of existence and mortality.

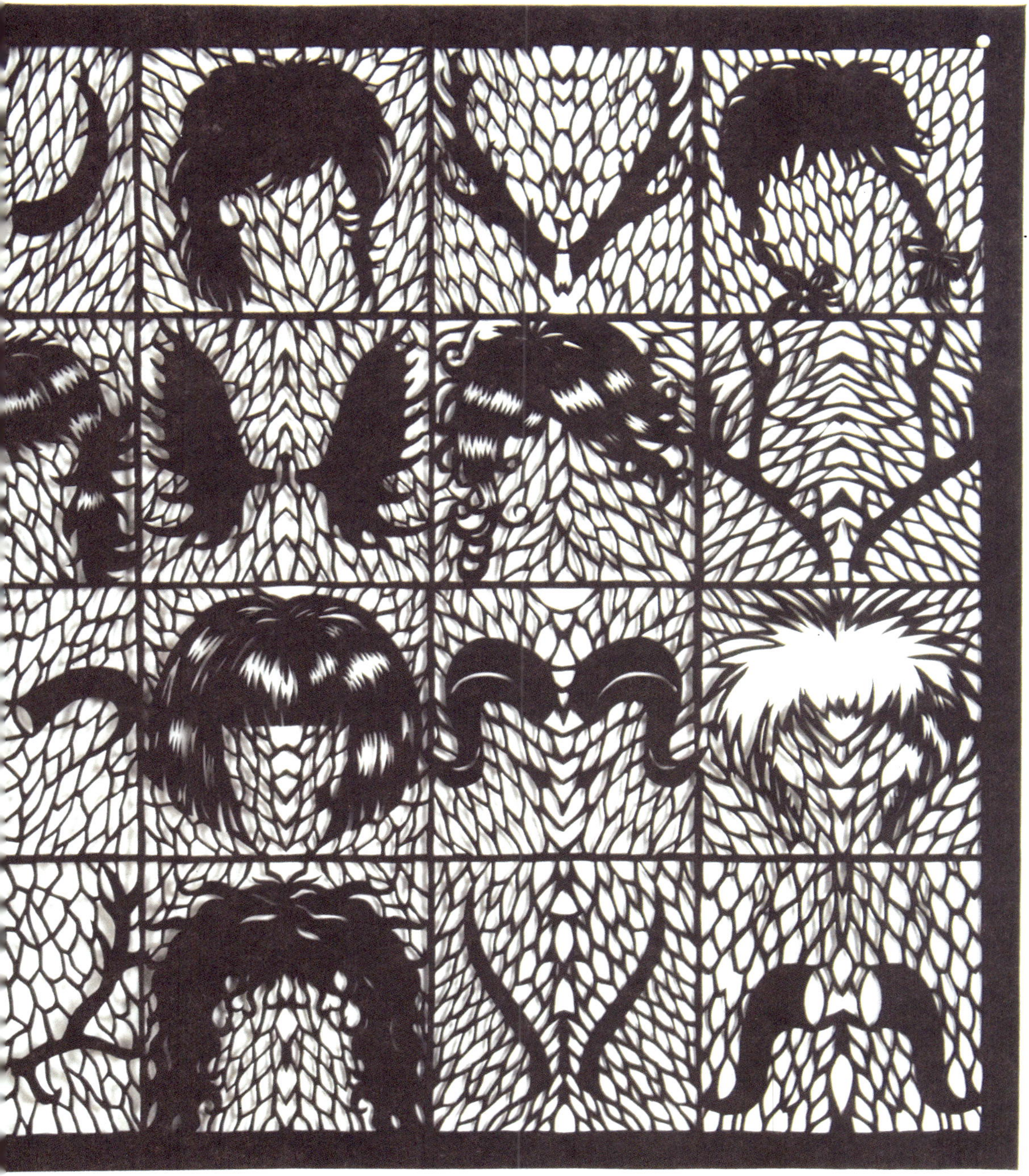

3 Horns & Wigs. Hand-cut black paper, 2005.

4

4 Vanitas. Hand-cut paper with watercolour, 2004-05.

1

Aoyama Hina

Japan & France

Aoyama Hina creates intricate paper-cuts with just a simple pair of scissors. Born in Yokohama, Japan, the artist now resides in Ferney Volaire in the east of France, and has been working on her paper cuts since 2000. Hina's passion lies in creating the finest cuts in paper that are beyond the level of time needed to make lace by needle. Hina does not follow "traditional methods" of paper-cutting but is instead "trying to create a mixture of the traditional and modern styles" with her "super-fine lacy paper-cutting technique."

1 Baudelaire. 60gsm Black paper, 2007.

2

2 Kirie. 60gsm Black paper, 2007.

1

2

Emma van Leest

Australia

A paper-cutting artist from Melbourne, Australia, Emma van Leest's work is labour intensive, descending from a tradition of domestic craft-making approaches which demand skill, labour and the meditative dedication of the artisan. The artist, who has held a residency at Sanskriti Kendra in Delhi, India, references her images from different cultural sources, including Chinese comic books, Javanese shady puppets, medieval illustrations and botanical drawings.

1~3 **The Dowsed Heart I-III.** 200gsm cartridge paper, 2008. The ancient art of divining for water was known as "dowsing"; this image is filled with witches, possessed animals, old timber homes, Victorian lace and bare trees.

3

2

2 To Dream in Waking Life. Synthetic paper, 2008.

1

Adriane Colburn
United States

Adriane Colburn's large-scale paper-cuts are no easy feat considering the themes she works with. Her constructions depict places of the world not usually accessible to the urban dweller's eye. Subterranean systems of the city such as sewer and water systems, networks of pipes that facilitate the taken-for-granted functions of modern societies, or systems found in the natural world such as the anatomy of a microscopic organism, are analysed and systematised by Colburn into a visual map.

An artist based in San Francisco with a Master of Fine Arts from Stanford University, Colburn started out as an artist who worked mostly digitally. Her first cut works used digital photographs and a laser camera. "I quickly realised, however, that I could work faster and more spontaneously if I did things by hand," says Colburn.

Honing her paper-cutting skills over a period of eight years, Colburn works confidently in "mapping" out these complex systems on paper, then building her installation in components and assembling the composition in the gallery. These visual "maps" attempt to organise the shifting environments of the urban and natural landscape; the resulting images are "abstractions that can be both informative and/or ambiguous".

1 **Piped In, Hooked On II.** Fabriano Tiziano pastel paper, aluminum, ink and latex paint, 2008. The installation investigates the processes of the oil industry in its submerged network of pipelines and refineries.

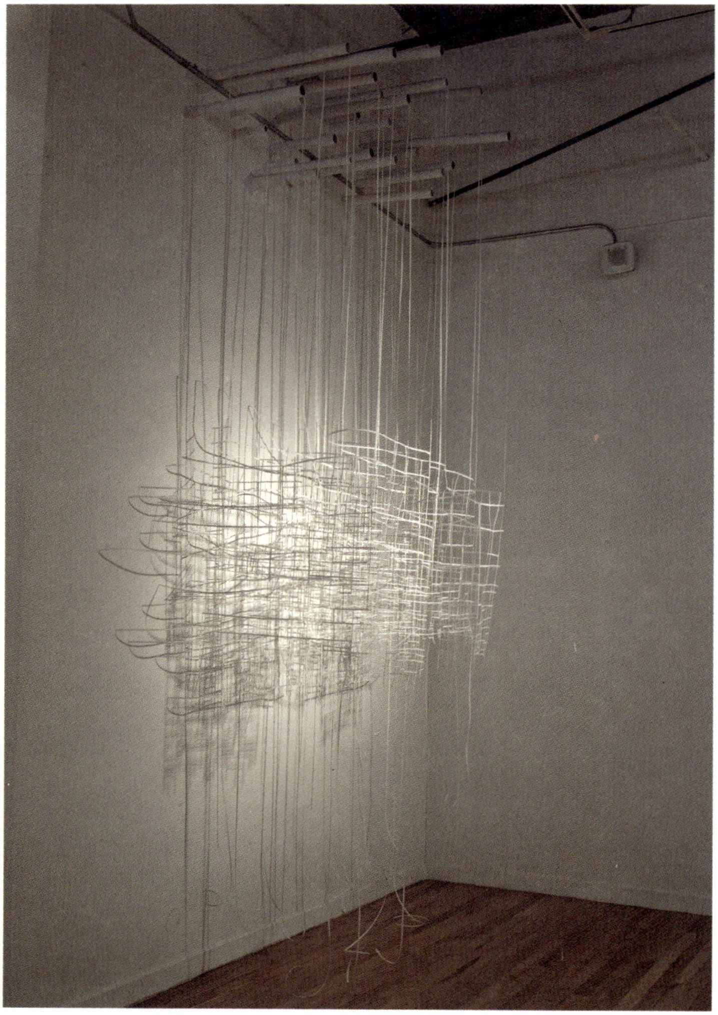

2

3

What were your biggest challenges dealing with paper?
The biggest problem has to do with the fragility of paper, how humidity affects the material during exhibition and storage; and also the effect of gravity due to the scale of my work. My biggest enemy is wind. In small quantities, it can provide a very graceful motion to the light paper works; in large quantities it can wreak havoc.

It must be painstaking work to hand cut paper to depict the complex systems in the natural and urban landscape. Why did you choose paper as a medium to express your theme?
Paper is a natural material since my work mostly revolves around issues in cartography and drawing. Making the cut work is tied to the idea that we make maps through a rigid editing process that leaves out all information except that which we want to illuminate.

You make large-scale installations with paper. How do the works hold up without breaking?
The strength of the paper I use is very high in comparison to its weight. For this reason, it is much stronger than one would guess. Those little strands are not actually holding much when it comes to mass. Also, when the paper has a grain, I try to work with that to increase strength.

2 **The Works.** Fabriano Tiziano pastel paper, 2006. This work references city maps and urban public works systems.

3 **Morning Becomes Parasympathetic.** Fabriano Tiziano pastel paper and ink, 2005. This large paper cut-out references the parasympathetic nervous system and illustrates the human body's inner workings.

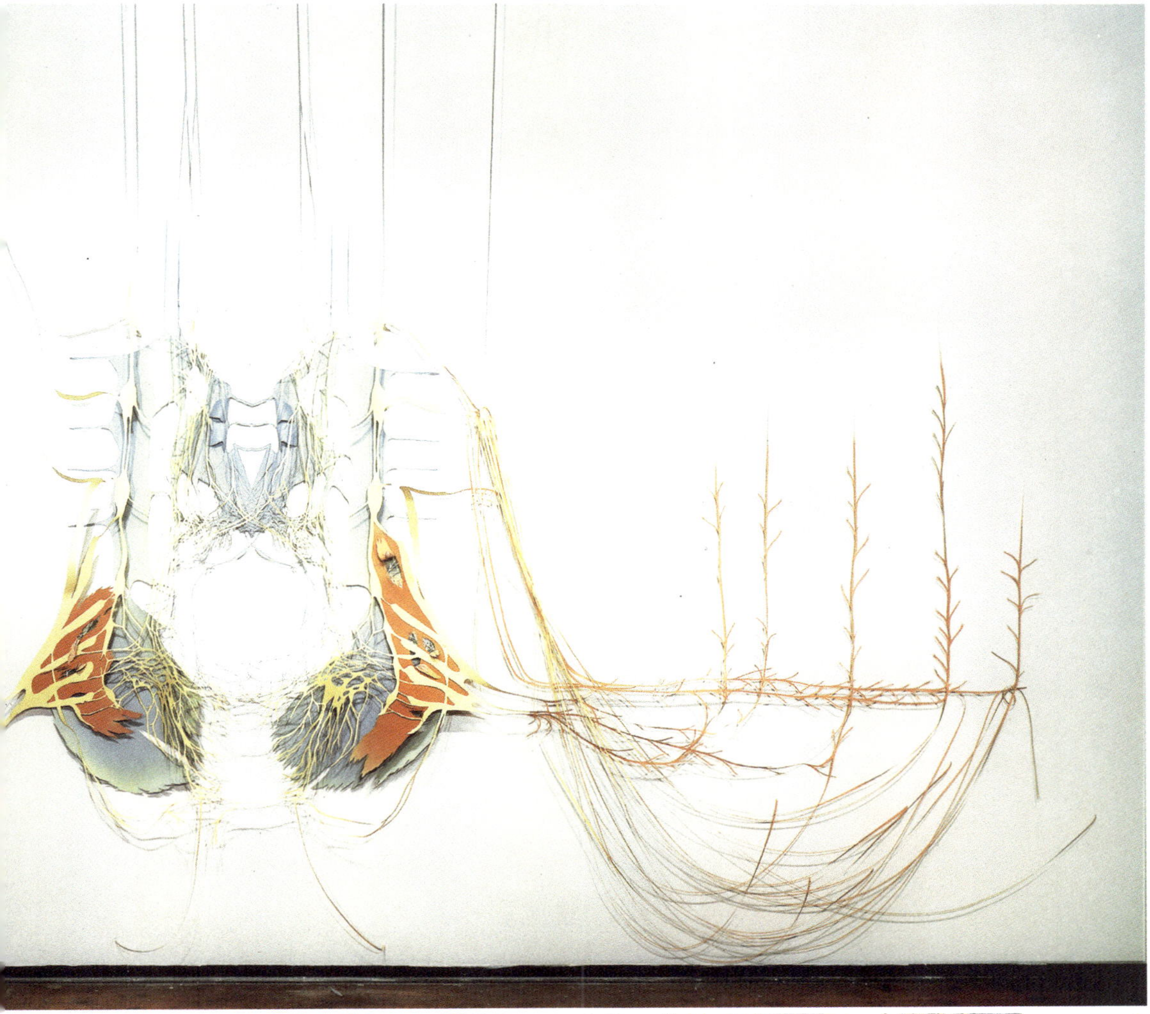

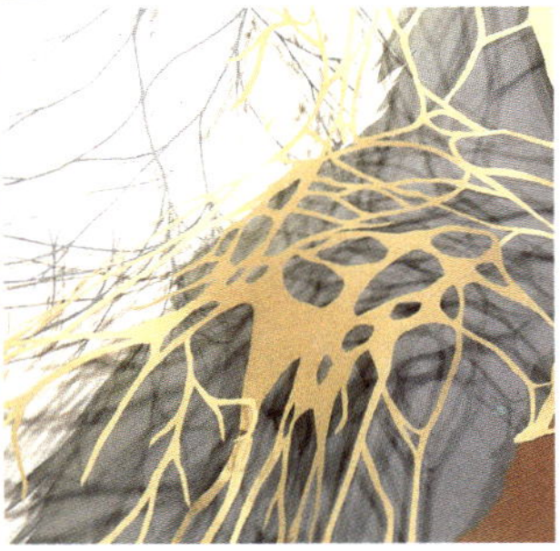

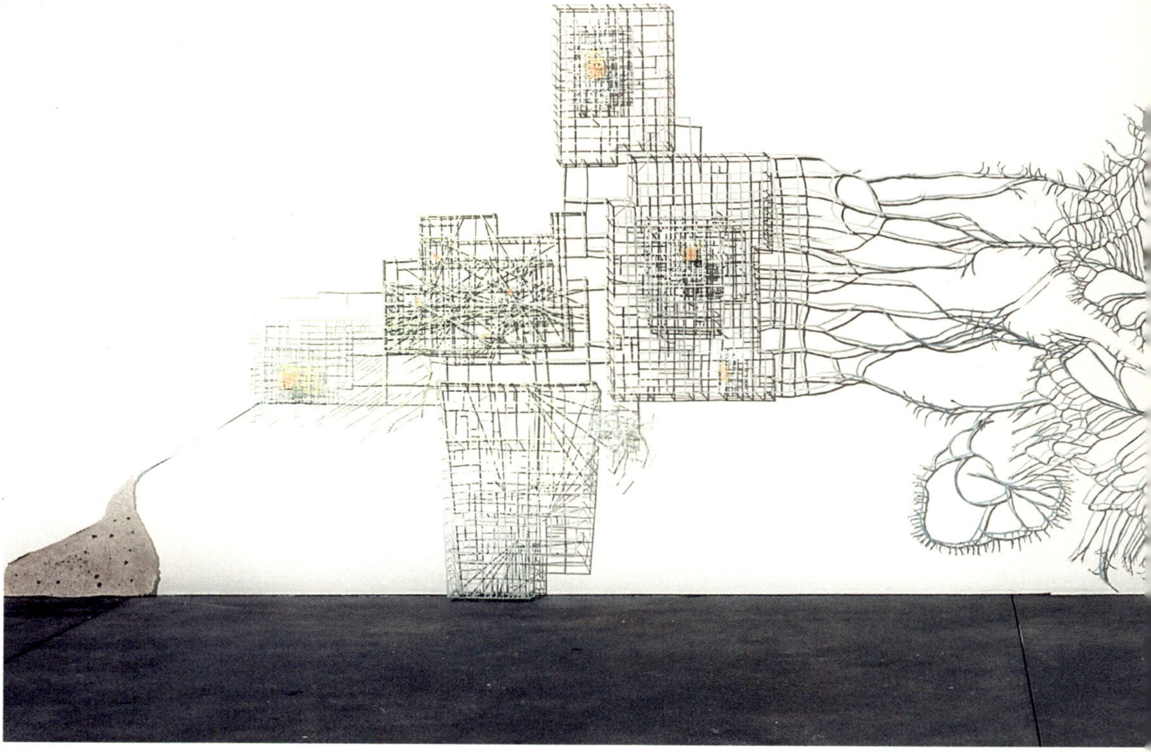

4

4 **Just Below (Sewer to Bay).** Rice paper, Fabriano Murillo paper, Fabriano Tiziano paper and ink, 2005. Displayed at the Yerba Buena Center for the Arts in San Francisco, this installation charts the sewer system from the museum to the Bay area of the city.

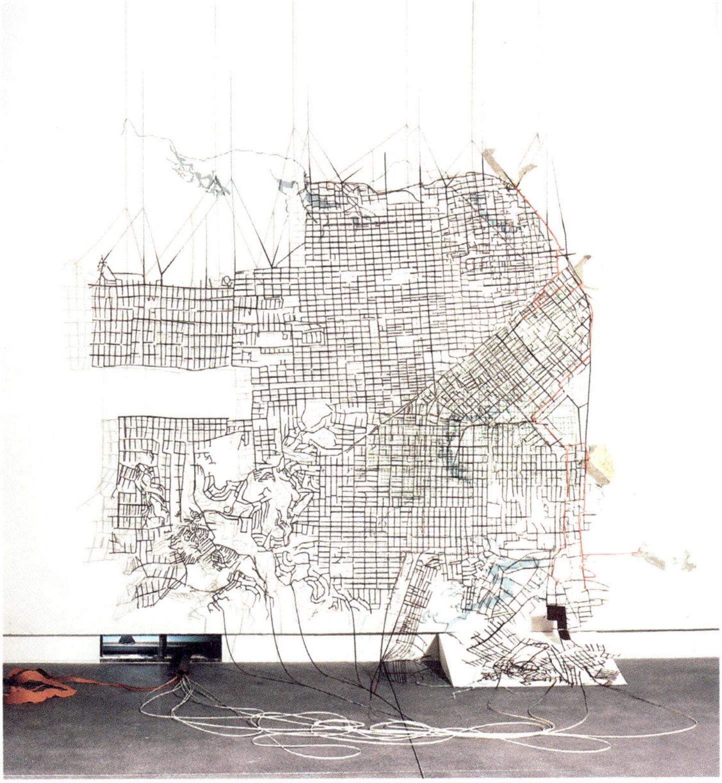

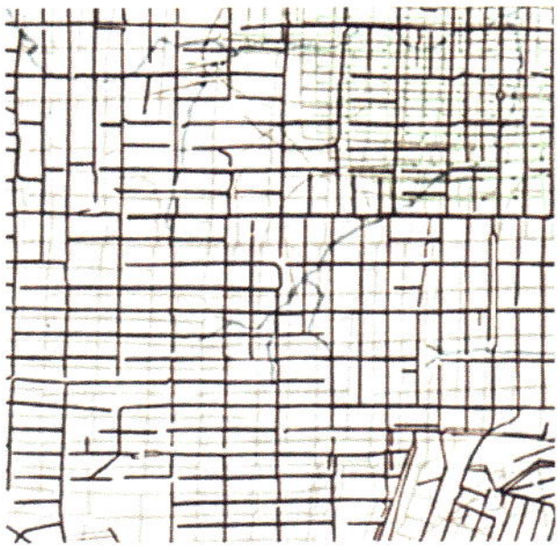

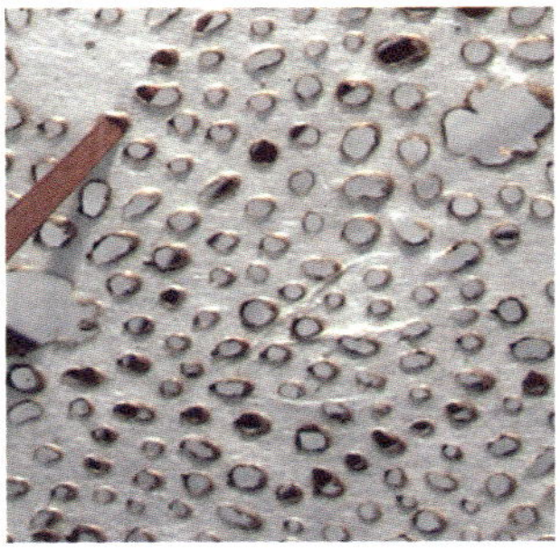

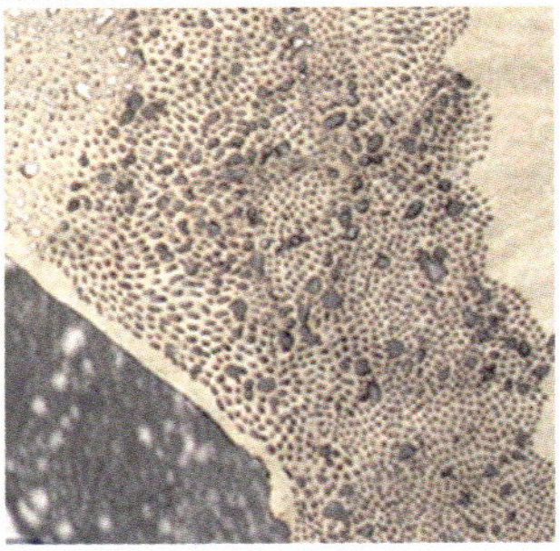

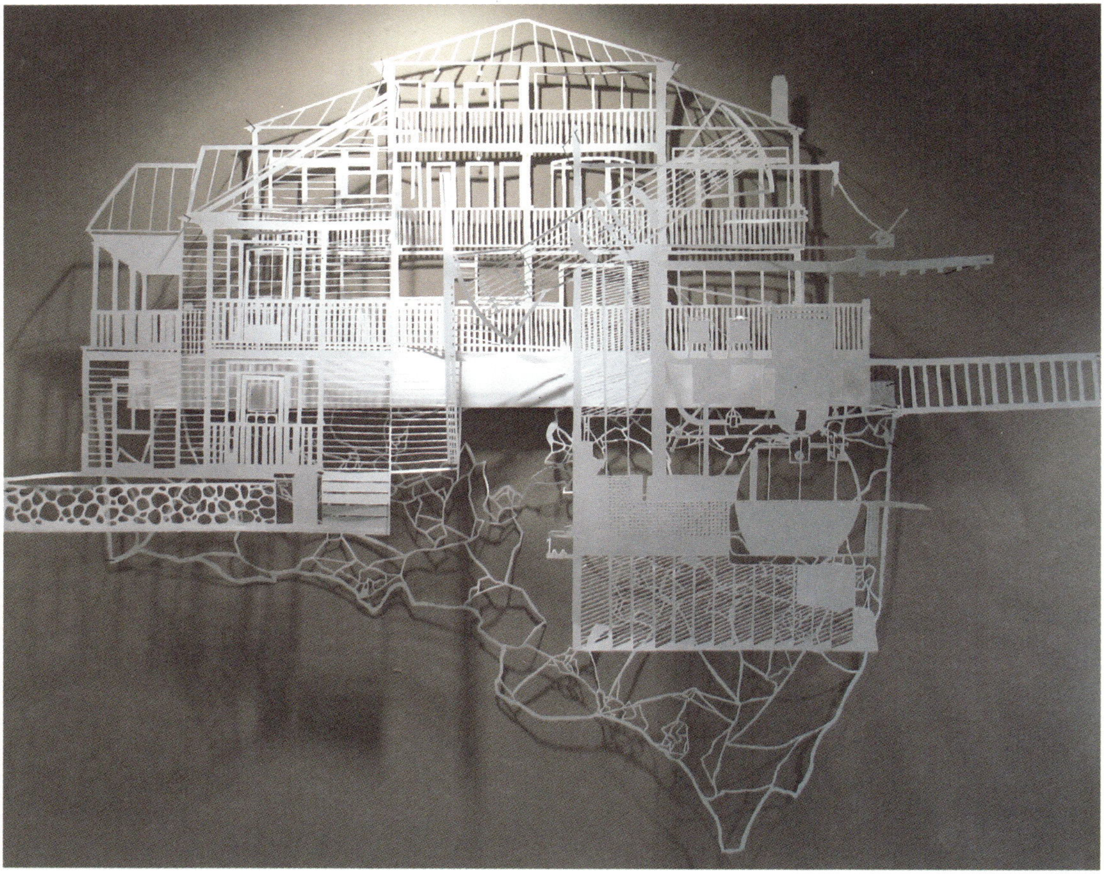

1

2

Laura Cooperman
United States

American artist Laura Cooperman was born to a family or architects; at age eight, she probably became the youngest subscriber of *Architectural Digest*. Creating elaborate structures, floor plans and arranging household objects were part of her childhood, and those hours of play are today witnessed in her paper-cuts which carry a sense of architectural monumentality, intricate layering and organisation.

1~3 **Breach.** Arches paper, metal rods, gears and chain, 2006. A paper-cut series which plays on the various definitions of the word "breach".

3

Shannon Rankin

United States

Instead of the typical paper-cutting method – a subtractive approach where defined areas are cut away to form an image – Shannon Rankin builds these images with layer upon layer of vellum, like a chef carefully organising a multi-layered cake. The interdisciplinary artist cuts endless organic shapes from folded vellum and layers the varying forms until they are 'connected' into a graphic by stippling and embroidery.

The *Simpling Series* is based on the Rorschach Inkblot test and loosely on the art of simpling, an early form of herbalism. Rankin chose to work without the distraction of colour in order to allow the forms, symbolising subconcious thoughts, to reveal themselves. Her paper-cuts in the *Simpling Series* search for the connections between anatomy and botany and the images combine the visual elements of human anatomy and plants.

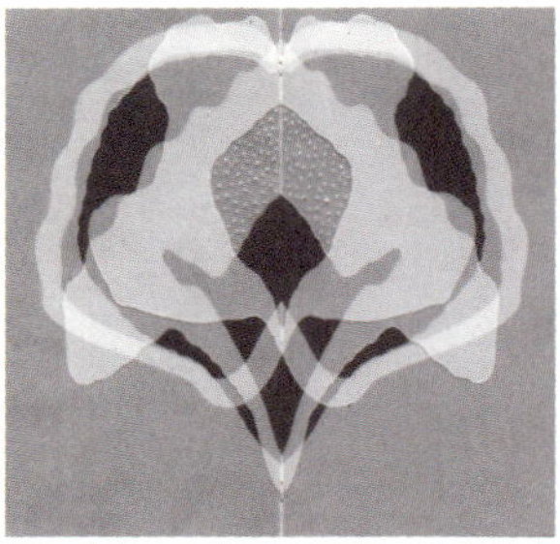
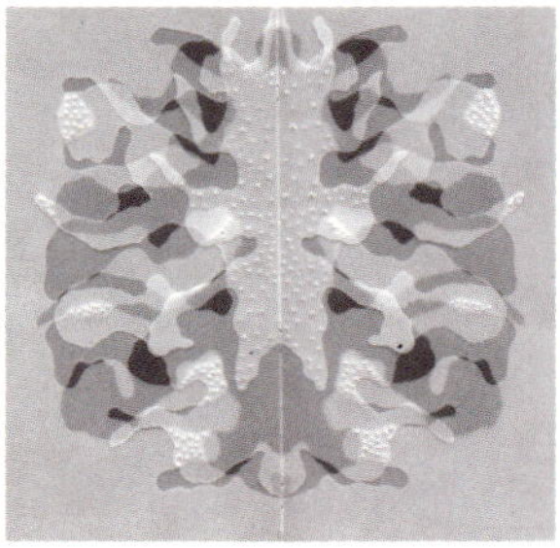
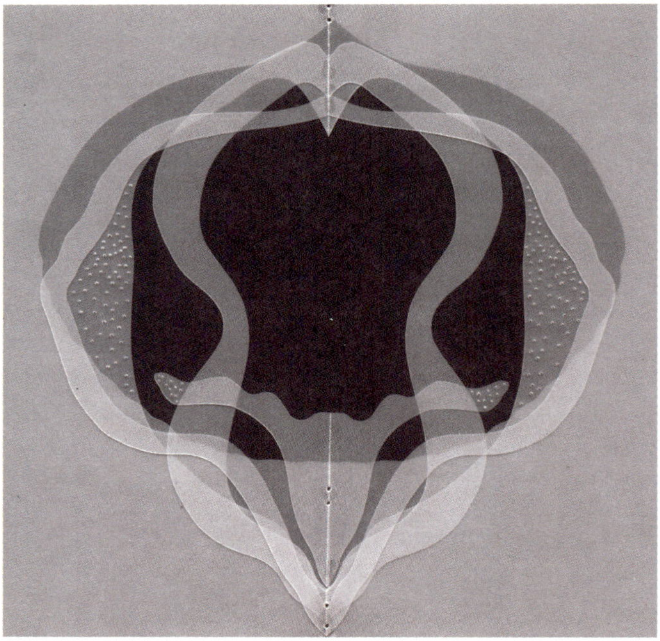

1

1 **Simpling Series.** Vellum, thread, monofilament and glue, 2006. The translucency of vellum allows for subtle shifts in value.

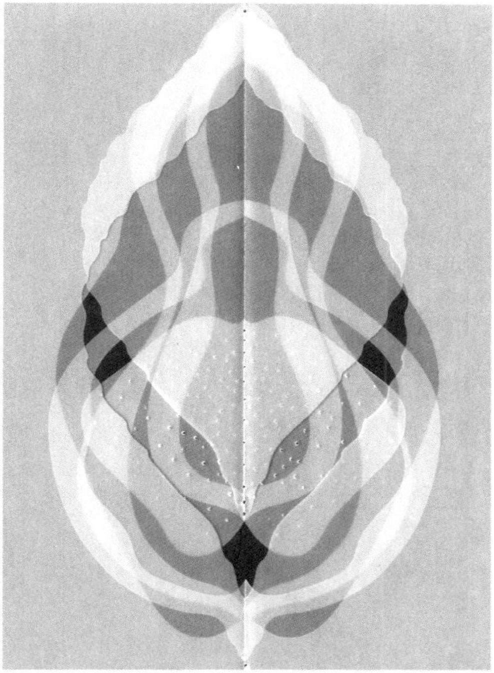

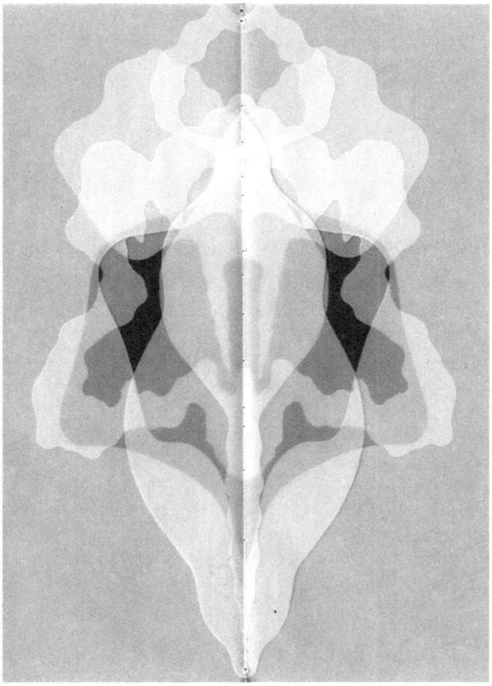

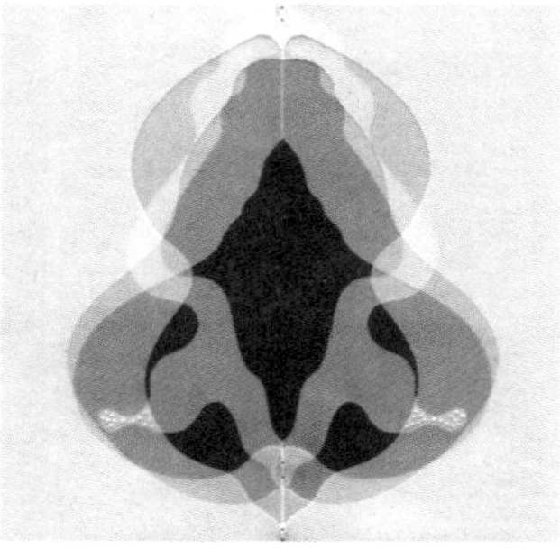

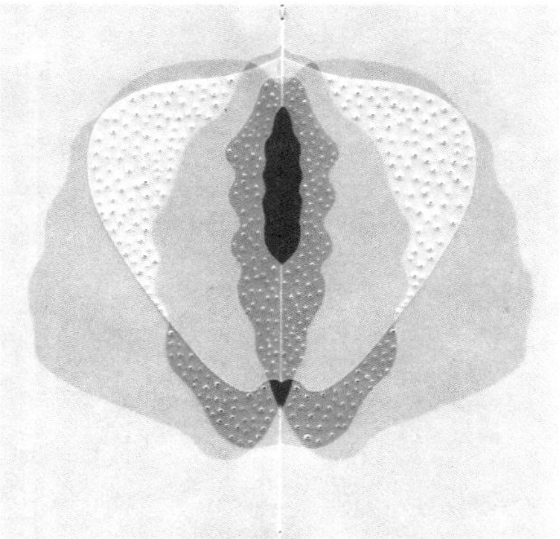

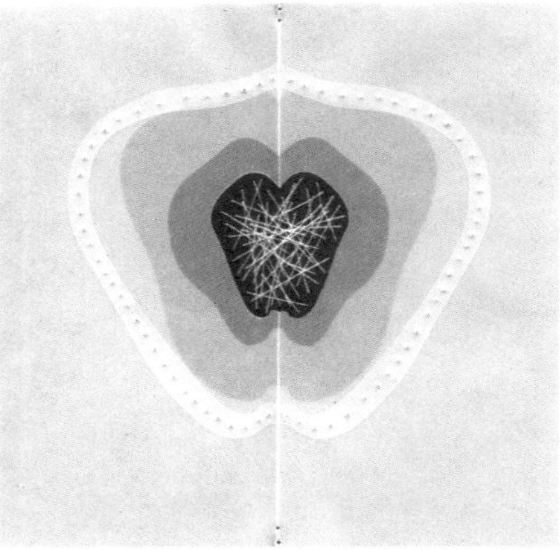

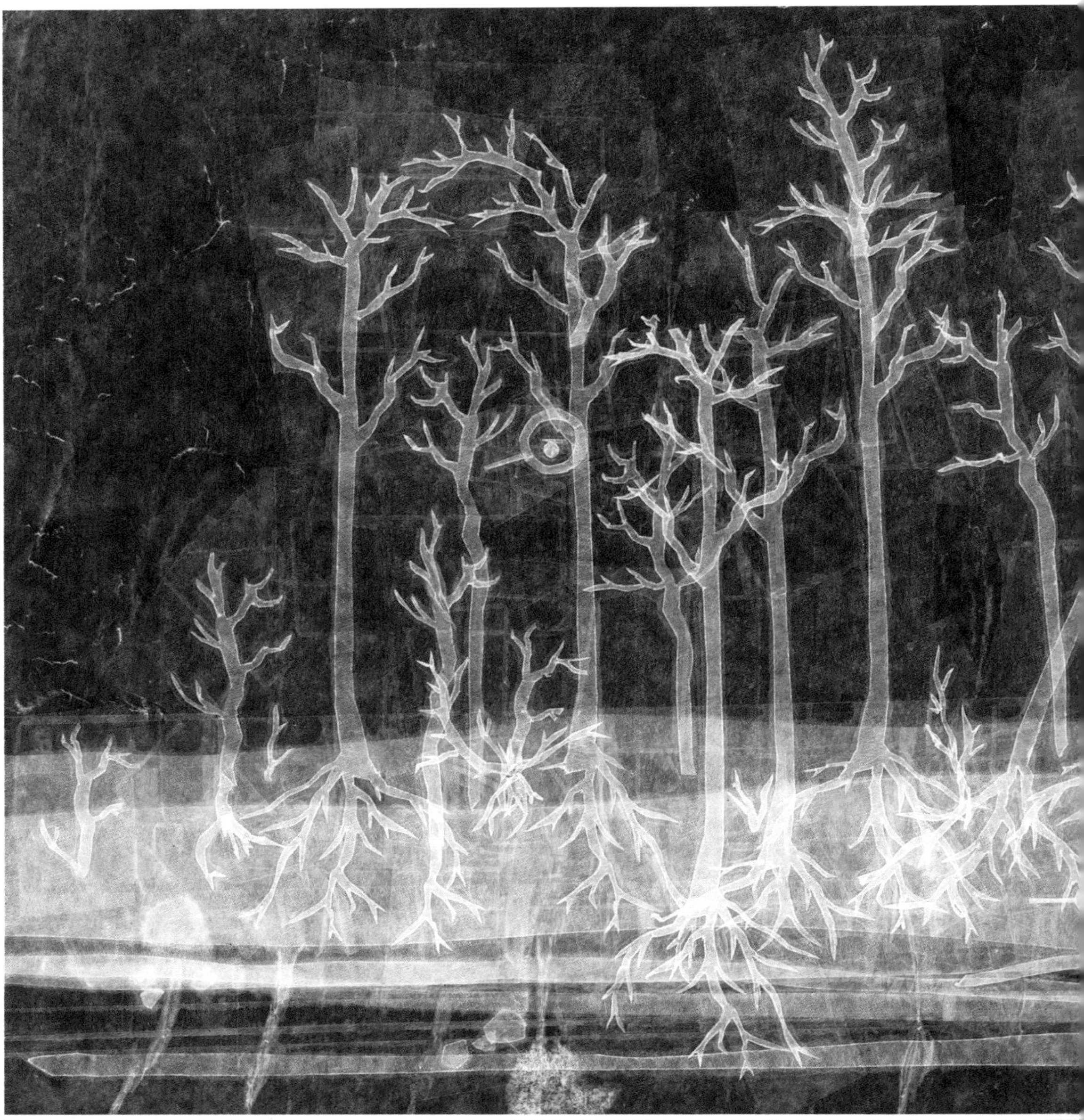

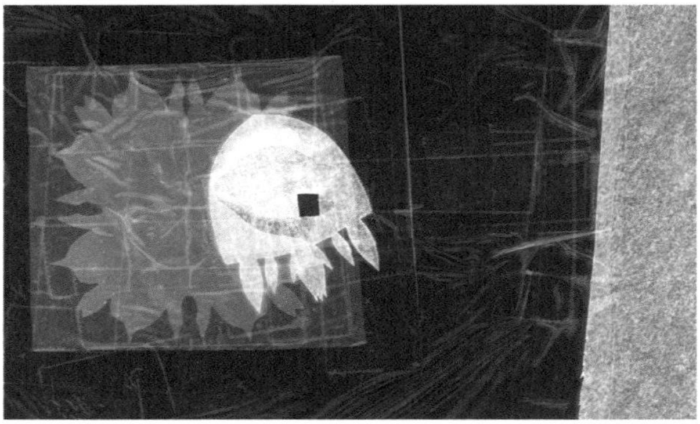

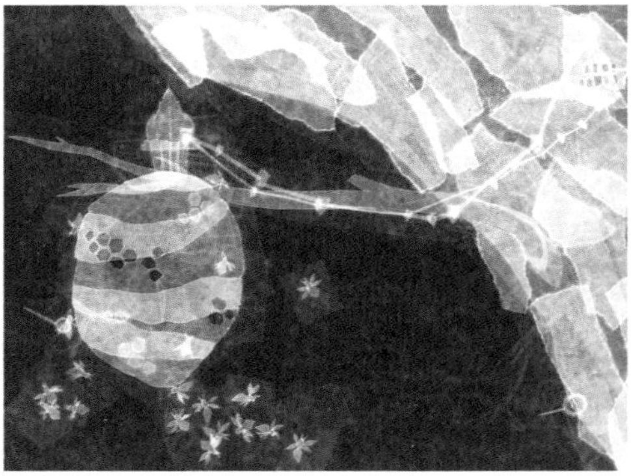

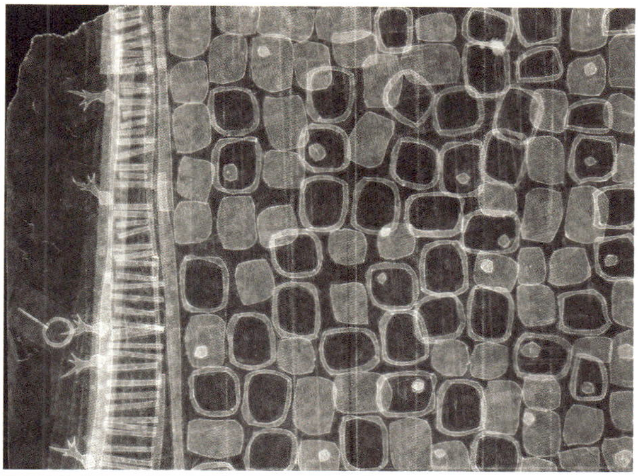

1

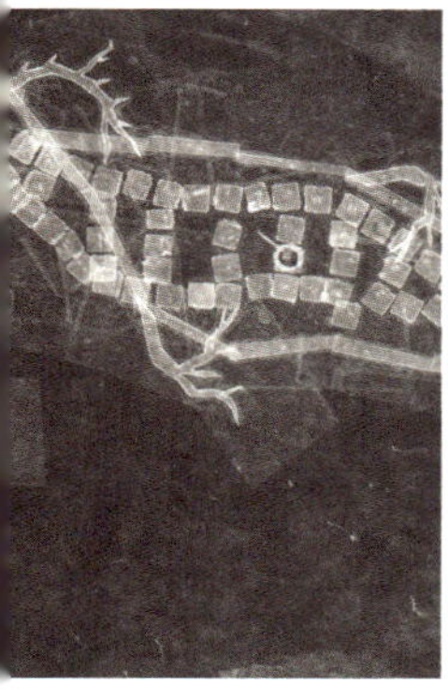

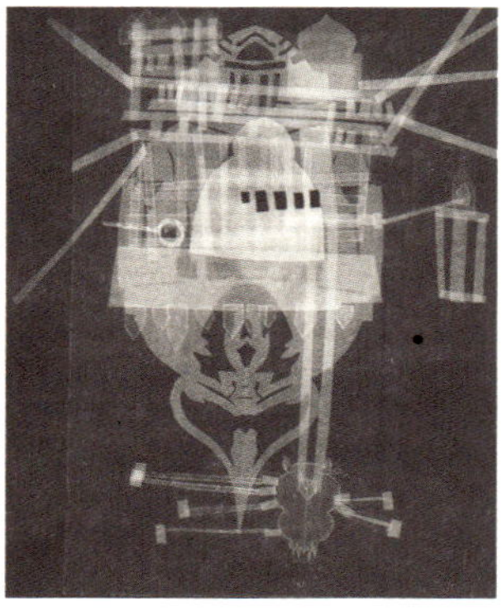

Greg Lendeck

United States

Greg Lendeck cuts out forms both solid and ghost-like, slowly, by hand, with an X-Acto knife. Working from a basic idea, he works intuitively and spontaneously to create haunting images with mysterious compositions, in essence, "assemblages of things that are and things that could be".

"The images represent separate moments but many of them have overlapping components that help illustrate the inter-connectedness and layered complexity of nature," explains the artist who resides in upstate New York. Using wax paper, which allows for variations in transparencies, Lendeck views *Pages of the Infinite* as pages "of an endless book that freeze-frames every moment within the infinite".

1 **Pages from The Infinite.** Wax paper, vellum, glassine, tissue, clear or translucent tape, plastic sheet, plexiglass, year ongoing. According to Lendeck, wax paper possesses the perfect translucency and cuts smoothly.

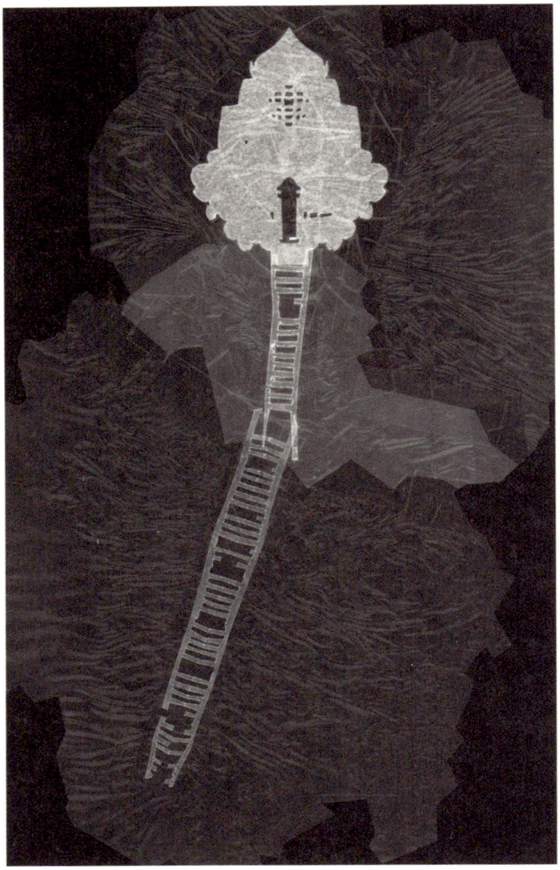

2

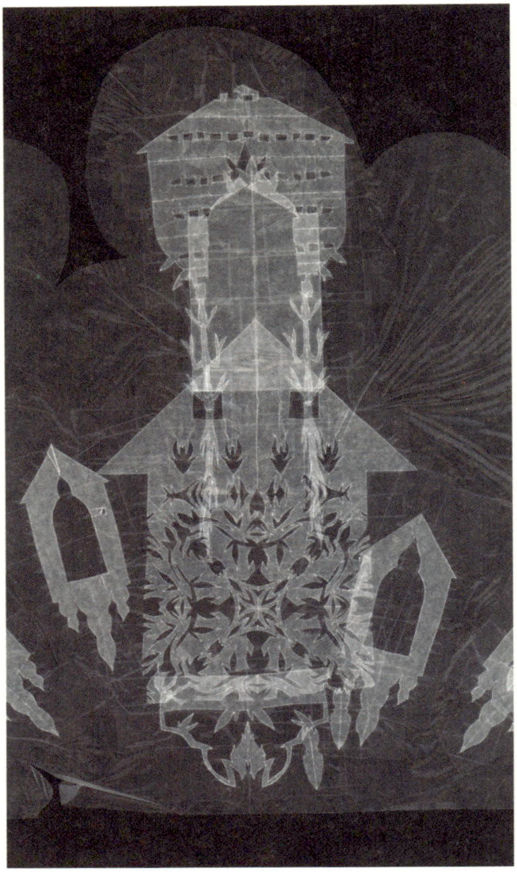

3

2~5 **Pages from The Infinite**. Wax paper, vellum, glassine, tissue, clear or translucent tape, plastic sheet, plexiglass, year ongoing. When layered, a strange three-dimensional effect occurs which is not visible in photographs.

4

5

1

Miriam Londoño
The Netherlands

Columbian artist Miriam Londoño works with language and uses written text in a calligraphic style to form images like a complex, mysterious script. By turning words into visual objects, Londoño's paper cuts are a kind of literal visual poetry, where the gaps and spaces in between give presence to a work of art.

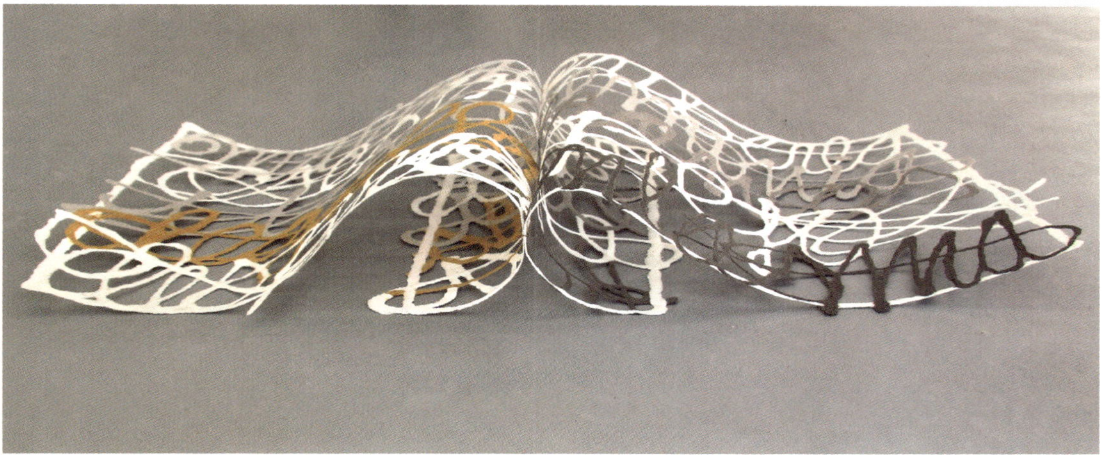

2

1 **Nets**. Handmade paper of cotton and flax, pigments and glue, 2007. The lines of the city landscape are made of paper.

2 **Book**. Handmade paper of cotton and flax, pigments and glue, 2006. The words written in this book have been transformed into paper. The words become a net of lines where the light dialogues with the words.

1

Robert Ryan

United Kingdom

"You can still do a lot with a small brain", or in the work of United Kingdom illustrator and paper-cut artist Robert Ryan, one can enchant with just a piece of paper and a cutting knife. Clients like *Vogue*, Liberty department store, Paul Smith, Roxy Quiksilver, Penguin and Random House have taken to his whimsical style of illustration which marries text and images. Random, off-kilter sentences ("I want to be live in Cundy Street and be seen as an individual" or "This bell will ring when we feel no hope") are woven into scenes and objects (bells, jugs, castles, birds, even underwear) creating tiny worlds of mystery and meaning.

Apart from working at his studio in East London, Ryan has also published a coffee-table book of his paper-cuts and screen-prints titled *This is For You*. In the summer of 2008, a friend offered him a store space on Columbia Street in East London. Six weeks later, Ryantown, a shop and gallery now gives customers a chance to purchase Ryan's intricate paper-cuts. "Because the store is only open weekends I decided to take it on, thinking it wouldn't be much work," shares Ryan, who produces fresh stock of paper-cuts for his store in small editions, "Little did I know!" Ryan makes the items in his studio while a manager runs Ryantown for him. A tiled mural on one of the walls in the shop will eventually be covered entirely with Ryan's work.

Working his illustrations into paper since 2002, in 2008, Ryan has worked on developing a ceramic range for Paul Smith, a children's book, illustrations for authors, handling an endless amount of inquiries and organising two exhibitions. Ryan proposes the craft of paper-cutting has become contemporary in context because of our rapidly computerised environment. "It's almost anti-technology. It simple rather than complex," says Ryan. It is perhaps a focus on simplicity (his reason for switching to paper-cutting) that underlies his creative process – "The simplest way of doing things is often the most effective."

2

1 Pants. Paper, 2004. For *The Museum of Us* exhibition.
2 Everything I Do. Paper, 2004. For *The Museum of Us* exhibition
3 We Don't Fly North. Paper, 2008.

WE DON'T FLY NORTH. WE DON'T FLY SOUTH. WE STAY
PUT RIGHT HERE. 365 DAYS A YEAR. YEAR IN YEAR OUT. THE
PEOPLE NEXT DOOR AND THE FLOOR
BELOW AND THE BUILDING NEXT
DOOR & THE BUILDING NEXT DOOR TO THAT
& THE WHOLE STREET AND THE
NEXT STREET AND THE NEXT STREET UNTIL IT
SEEMS AS IF EVERY BUILDING IN THE ENTIRE CITY
SEEMED TO JOIN ONTO ITS
NEIGH- BOUR TO MAKE
JUST ONE VAST SINGLE
BUILD- ING. WITH ONLY A SERIES
OF WALLS BETWEEN YOU AND EVERY OTHER PERSON IN
THE CITY. ONCE WE WERE JUST
NEIGH- BOURS. NOW WE
ARE FRIENDS. WE NEVER
TRAV- ELLED VERY FAR.
BUT WE WENT THE DISTANCE

3

HAPPY
XMAS
FROM
THE
QUARRY

5

6

7

4 **Xmas Card Lazercut for The Quarry.** 300gsm Colorplan by GF Smith, 2007. Xmas card laser cut for client in the film post-production industry, The Quarry, London.

5 **Lazercut desk calender.** 300gsm Colorplan by GF Smith, 2008. A promotional desk calendar given out to clients.

6 **Lazercut Magazine cover inset.** 300gsm Colorplan by GF Smith, 2004. An alternative lazercut magazine cover for *Amelia's* Magazine.

7 **Thank you card.** Screen-printed card with paper-cuts, 2007.

THIS BELL WILL RING WHEN THE LEAVES FALL
THIS BELL WILL RING WHEN YOU TAKE ME IN YOUR ARMS AND HOLD ME
THIS BELL WILL RING WHEN WE RUN FOR THE BUS
THIS BELL WILL RING WHEN THESE DAYS ARE GONE
THIS BELL WILL RING WH WE FEE NO HOP
THIS BELL WILL RING WHEN OUR TIME HAS COME
THIS BELL WILL RING WHEN WE ARE ALONE
THIS BELL WILL RING WHEN WE DREAM A DREAM OF GOOD
THIS BELL WILL RING WHEN PEOPLE SAY THAT WE ARE BORING

9

8 Bell Park. Paper, 2004. For *The Museum of Us* exhibition.
9 Cloughvase. Paper, 2004. For *The Museum of Us* exhibition.

1

Peter Callesen

Denmark

Danish artist Peter Callesen works mainly with the humble white paper in different objects, paper-cuts, installations and performances. His paper-cuts and sculptures are as much poetic performances and fantasy narratives as they are astounding feats of craft, wherein the "impossible becomes real". Castles, the Tower of Babel, cages, doves and ruins are just some images which populate this artist's romantic universe. The paper-cuts embody their own melancholy: each three-dimensional paper sculpture is stuck to a two-dimensional cut space on a piece of paper, suggesting the tragedy of never being able to escape one's origin.

A quick search on social networking website *Facebook* will take you to the Peter Callesen Appreciation Group, a telling indication of this artist's rising profile beyond the closed circles of art. "I think it is interesting that I am not only communicating within the established art scene, but also within a much bigger and very different sphere on the Internet," shares Callasen.

When asked to describe himself in any way, Callesen chooses to return to his cherished medium, "Maybe Peter Callesen is a paperman, just made out of paper. Maybe the house he lives in, the town he lives in, everything that surrounds him is just made out of paper. And maybe all the paper is cut out from a big book of white blank pages that someone is reading right now."

1 **Distant Wish.** 115gsm Acid-free A4 paper and glue, 2006.
2. **All in All.** 115gsm Acid-free A4 paper and glue, 2006.

2

4

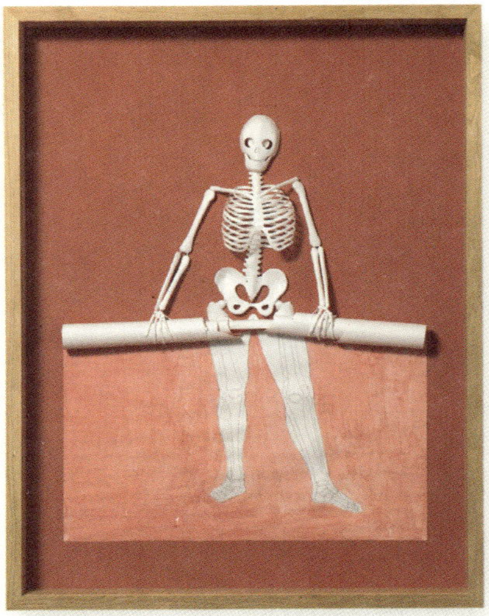

6

8

3

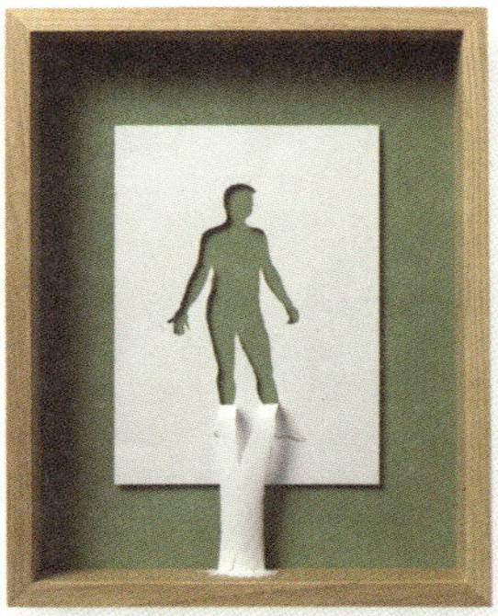

5

7

9

3 **Not as Fast as his Shadow**. 115gsm Acid-free A4 paper and goache paint in oak wood frame, 2008.

4 **Bound to be Free**. 115gsm Acid-free A4 paper and goache paint in oak wood frame, 2008.

5 **Liquidated Man**. 115gsm Acid-free A4 paper and goache paint in oak wood frame, 2008.

6 **Cut to the Bone II**. 115gsm Acid-free paper in oak wood frame, 2008.

7 **Hanging Image**. 115gsm Acid-free paper and goache paint and pencil in oak wood frame, 2008.

8 **Struggle**. 115gsm Acid-free A4 paper and goache paint in oak wood frame, 2008.

9 **Crying my Eyes Out**. 115gsm Acid-freeA4 paper and goache paint and pencil in oak wood frame, 2008.

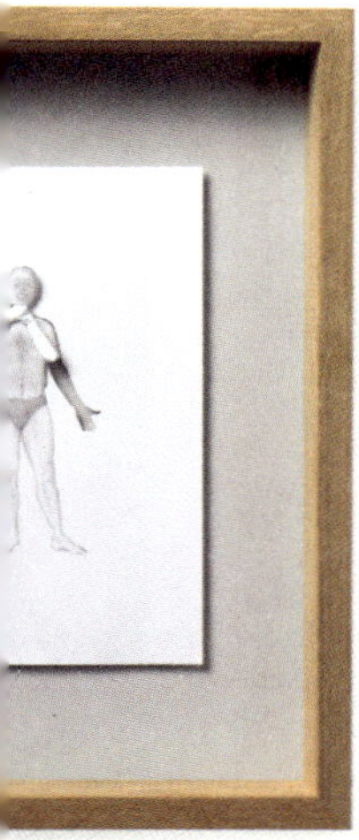

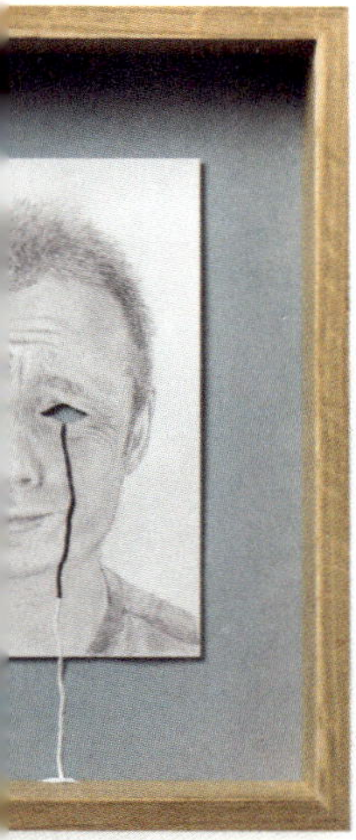

You started using A4 paper in a performance in 2003. What happened then?
I was invited to the performance festival *Amorph* in Helsinki to do a castle performance. I decided to make a sheet of paper that people could cut, fold, and glue into their own little castle. But because I wanted it to be an image dealing with the impossible and illusions, I made the instructions and the cut-out lines for the castle so small, complicated and detailed that it would be an impossible task. Six months after the show, it occurred to me to have a go at making parts of the castle – just for fun. It turned out to be nearly possible to do. The idea for the small A4-sculptures was thus conceived.

Why have you continued working with just the white A4 paper?
I still find it interesting to work with the A4 sheet of paper. It is probably the most common and consumed media used for carrying information. We rarely notice the actual materiality of the A4 paper. The thin white paper gives the paper sculptures a fragility that underlines the tragic and romantic theme of my works.

That frailty seems to connect to the narratives and themes in your paper-cuts – fairytales, childhood memories, dreams, loss and fragility.
I think there is an obvious connection between the thin, white paper and its fragility. On a more literal level, the paper also directly refers to narratives, because paper used to be the most common media to communicate stories. What I may be doing is to empty the paper of all its information and point towards the potential stories within the blank paper. You could argue that the whiteness and emptiness of the paper points towards something almost sublime, which to me, relates to dreams.

You also tell a story by the way your paper sculptures are "stuck" to a cut area on the sheet of paper.
The paper-cut sculptures explore the probable and magical transformation of the flat sheet of paper into figures that expand into the space surrounding them. The negative and absent two-dimensional space left by the cuts contrasts with the three-dimensional reality, even though the figures are still stuck to their origin without the possibility of escaping it. In that sense, there is also an aspect of something tragic in many of the cuts.

It's a pessimistic thought – that one can never truly be free from one's origin. Is there a sense of hope in your work?
If there is a sense of hope in the work, maybe it would be the recognition of a feeling or experience, for instance, of being stuck without the possibilities of moving – but this may be presented in a way we have never seen before. I think that interesting art is the recognition of something we have never seen before.

Have you noticed a growing interest in using paper as a medium?
I actually did not notice this until a few years ago. But maybe it has to do with the fact that our world is becoming increasingly digitalised and disconnected from the concrete and physical. Maybe that is why we feel a need to return to something physical, something we can feel with our hands. To me, something handwritten has another more important and more beautiful meaning than something written on a computer. I do not believe we can live in a completely virtual world. It is also interesting that even though computers would supposedly result in a paper-free society, today, we seem to consume more paper than ever.

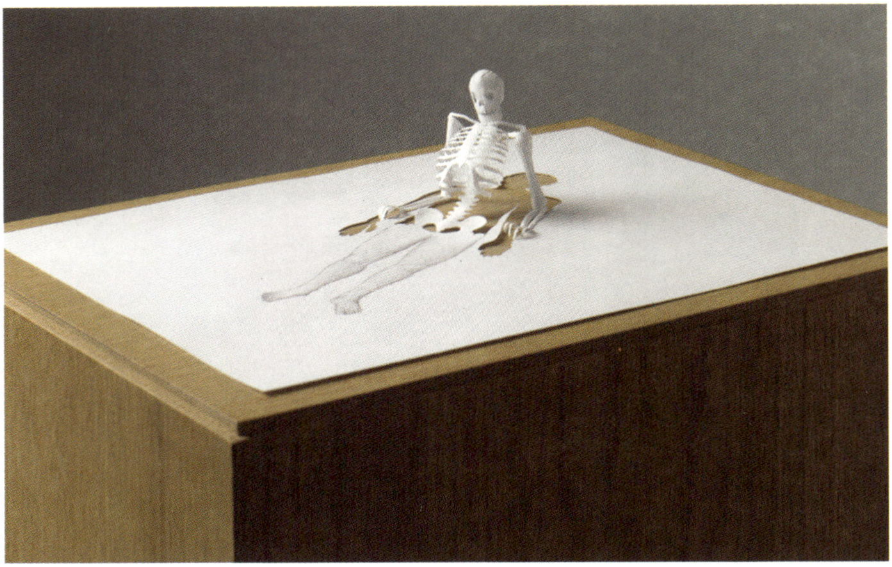

10

11

12

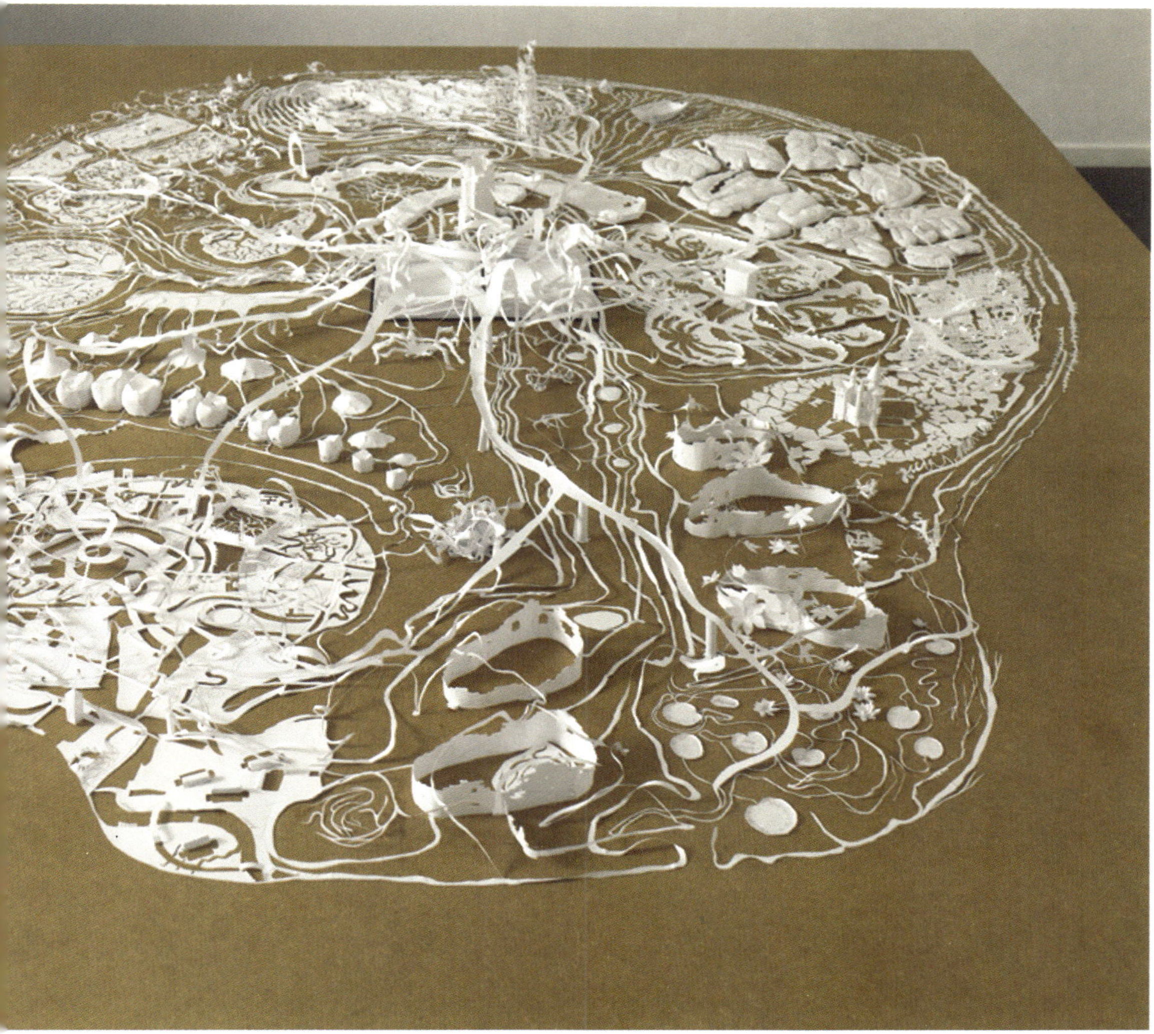

10 **Half Way Through.** 115gsm Acid-free A4 paper, pencil, and glue, 2006.
11 **Eismeer.** 80gsm Acid-free A4 paper and glue, 2006.
12 **White Diary.** 115gsm Acid-free paper, pencil and sketch book, 2008.

13

13 Snowballs. Acid free A4 80gsm paper and glue, 2005.

Arty Objects

Craft is the new collectable.

If you believe handicrafts to be the domestic past-time of retired ladies or a hobby with little relevance for design, these sculptural paper works will challenge your preconceptions. These days, paper craft is no longer limited to handmade papers or papier-mâché or art books. Paper leaves its traditional usage as a carrier for text to become a raw material for building objects and sculptures, taking the paper medium into the third-dimension.

Regarding the tactility of paper as its most important quality, rather than being a material for writing or printing, artists and designers are making paper works that bring to life the medium's physicality. *Arty Objects* showcases an eclectic range of paper objects from mathematical paper architecture, to paper notepads designed as sculptures, to books turned into theatrical sets, to tiny paper objects made from Japanese *washi* paper. *Arty Objects* also celebrates the book as a sculptural object, and its connection with the viewer as a work of art. These one-of-a-kind paper works in *Arty Objects* inspire with their creativity, beauty and by helping us to view this everyday material with fresh eyes and new perspectives.

Red Spout. Cardboard, wire and paint, 2006. By Ferry Staverman.
Yellow Head with Six Hearts. Cardboard, wire and paint, 2007.
By Ferry Staverman.

Cybèle Young

Canada

As a child, Cybèle Young made miniature farms. Today, the Canadian artist has perfected the art of small things through her interests in sculpture, installation and printmaking. Known for miniature paper sculptures, some of which can be as small as a mere 0.5 by 0.5 centimetres, the work is "physically challenging as it is very precise and specific." Young adds, "I have to take care of my neck, arms and eyes through exercise and physiotherapy."

Her sculptures are a grab bag of raincoats, pots, pans, cashiers, handbags, sofas – mundane objects from the ordinary moments of life. Using fine Japanese paper, she makes delicate prints with intricate copperplate etchings and chine-collé on the sculptures. "I'm very lucky because Nancy Jacobi has her business right here in Toronto," comments Young on the founder of The Japanese Paper Place in Toronto, the largest exporter of Japanese paper outside Japan. Young professes a fondness for traditional handmade Japanese paper, *washi*, especially paper made from *kozo* or *gampi* fibres for their incredible strength – "I have squished sculptures under my desk chair and was later able to revive it" – and the way her prints turn out wonderfully on these fine Japanese paper.

1

2

1 **Did You Pack A Lunch**. Japanese paper, 2005. Approximately 2.5 × 5 × 1 inches.

2 **You Won't Find It Here**. Japanese paper, 2007. A framed work, approximately 48 × 48 × 3 inches.

3

4

3 **Eight Pairings**. Japanese paper, 2006. A framed work, approximately 9 × 54 × 2 inches.

4 **Where's My List?** Japanese paper, 2004. A framed work, approximately 21 × 17 × 3 inches.

5 **We Found It Over There**. Japanese paper, 2006. Approximately 7 × 8 × 1 inches.

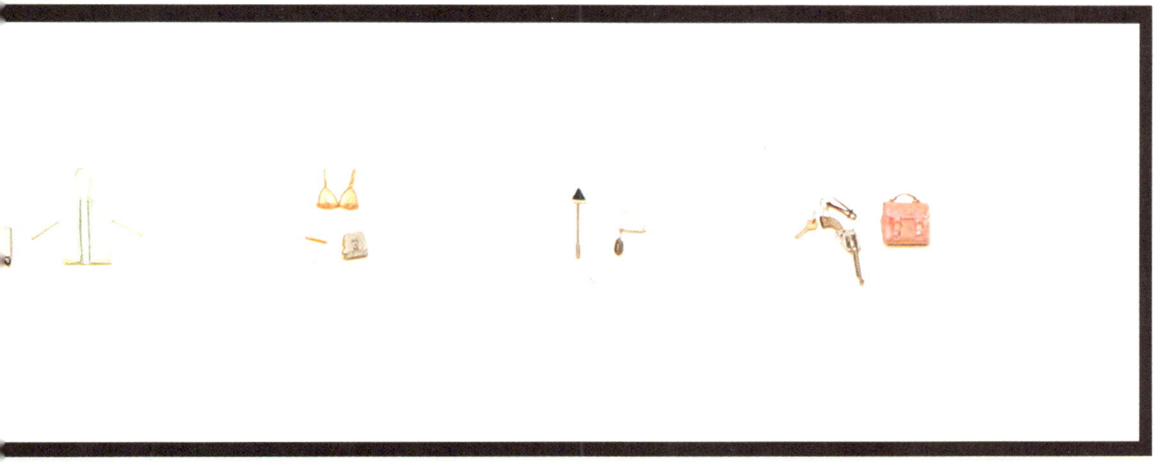

5

6

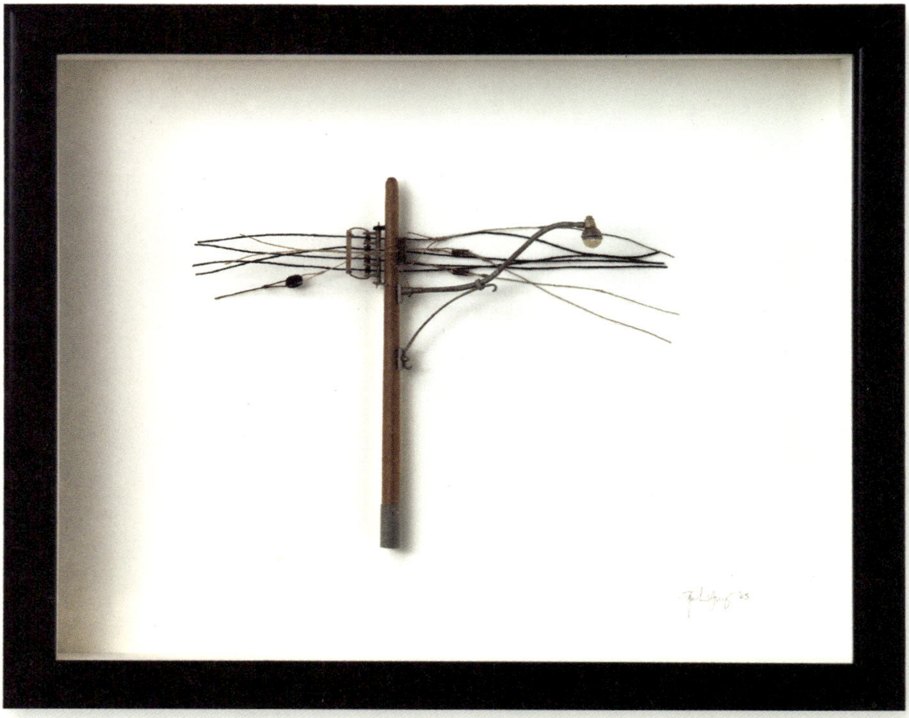

7

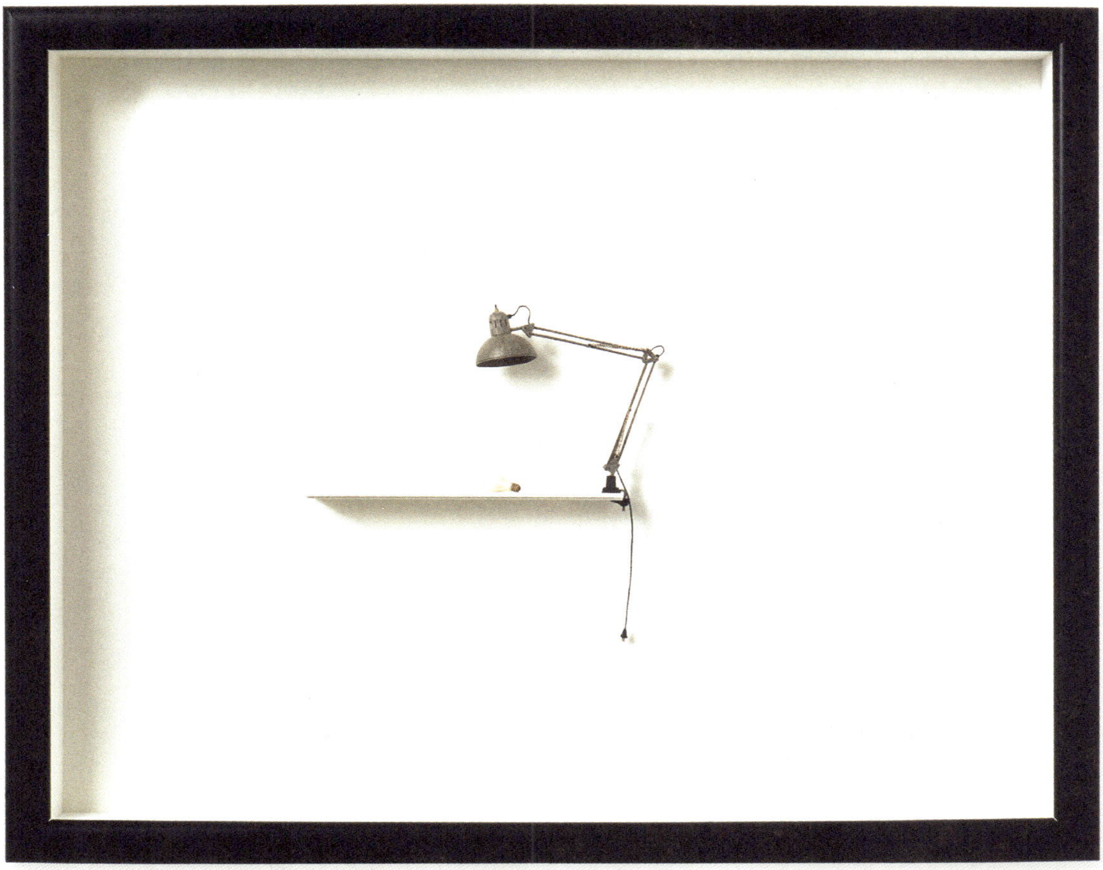

8

6 **Limited Options.** Japanese paper, 2005. A framed work, approximately 12 × 18 × 3 inches.

7 **That Was Last Week.** Japanese paper, 2006. A framed work, approximately 12 × 35 × 3 inches.

8 **I Thought I Heard Something.** Japanese paper, 2004. A framed work, approximately 17 × 21 × 3 inches.

1

2

3

Lizzie Buckmaster Dove

Australia

Australian artist Lizzie Buckmaster Dove makes three-dimensional paper constructions by folding and cutting books. The modified books allow the reader to look at its pages in a different way. Buckmaster Dove presents her works in complex formations: books on stands, in museum-like cases, and in miniscule tins, which reference the framework of scientific illustrations and cataloguing of natural history. Buckmaster Dove's love for the physicality of books – their texture, density, smell, and the movement of the pages – has led her to explore the beauty and intimacy of turning this everyday item into a beautiful object.

1 **A Disappearing Song.** Found printed paper, 2008.
2 **Wildflowers.** Found printed paper, tobacco tin and paint, 2007.
3 **Cacophony: Fleet Flicker Flight Fancy.** Folded paper book, 2007. A book construction created by folding with a view of birds in the Australian bush as they appear.

1

2

Kylie Stillman

Australia

After studying Painting at the Royal Melbourne Institute of Technology, Australian artist Kylie Stillman began working with found objects and domestic materials like books, Venetian blinds and plywood to create a set of unusual sculptures. Removing parts of the original material with a scalpel, Stillman carves out birds and plants from the pages of books and paper stacks. Stillman enjoys the process of "reversing the process in which positive images are made" through the act of trimming away which gives a potted plant form in the books.

Stillman, who exhibits these book sculptures at unique artist-run exhibition spaces throughout Melbourne, has found a fortuitous method of sourcing books for her art. "Some viewers offer me books from their own library, too precious to throw away but too outdated to serve its original purpose," says Stillman, "In this way I have been able to source some wonderful books and hear some of the stories of how these volumes came to be in their possession."

1 **Semiformal**. Book, 2004.
2 **Common Oak**. Books, dowel rods and wood base, 2007.

3

3 **Flock**. Books, 2007. A 4.5m bookshelf filled with encyclopedias and legal books is the largest book-based artwork made by Stillman installed at the Meat Market in Melbourne, Australia.

1

Holly Ormrod

United Kingdom

When Holly Ormrod began experimenting sculpturally with books, she was naturally nervous. "To this day, I never cut a book haphazardly. There is always a plan," says the Masters graduate in Book Arts from Camberwell College of Arts. Ormrod uses a meticulous method of cutting and assembly to construct stage-like sets and sculptures from books that literally spring to life when opened. Abandoned novels from second-hand shops are her mediumof choice as they "visibly communicate their own history" as a pre-loved item, quietly telling of the many hands they have passed through. Ormrod observes that people "get as close as possible and are often very quiet and contemplative" when viewing her work, generating an intimate relationship with her work. Ormrod has also made a short stop-motion animation film *Passage* with director Dan Richards which uses pioneering animation techniques using paper.

2

1~2 **Sonnet 104**. Book titled *The Complete Works of William Shakespeare*, 2006. A visual response to one of Shakepeare's sonnets, created entirely from a second-hand book, with a set-like and theatrical approach.

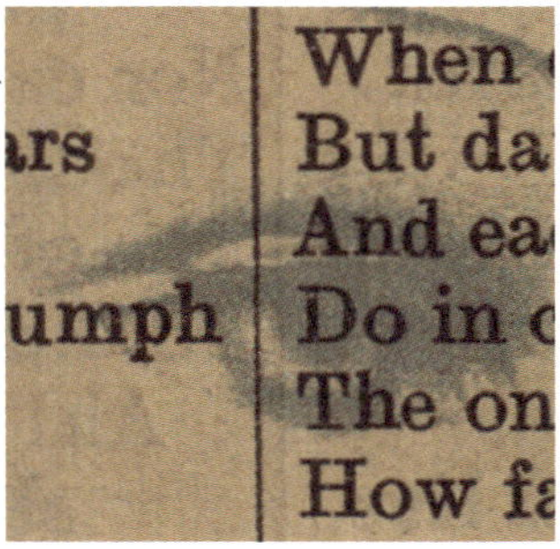
ars
umph
When
But da
And ea
Do in
The on
How fa

1

Cara Barer
United States

A random encounter with a discarded *Yellow Pages* led Texas artist Cara Barer to photograph the book's curled pages. Barer began developing the idea of books as sculptural objects, searching for methods to alter their appearance. Before photographing each book, she considers each book's physical properties – the quality of paper, colour, density, the contents and text within – before giving it a modified form. The book may be soaked in water for hours, curled up with hair rollers, or attached with Velcro, but all with pages carefully positioned to create books with fantastic forms.

Barer then photographs each book and prints them on 300gsm Crane Museo Portfolio Rag paper. All photos are in limited editions. Barer's work attempts to blur the lines between object, sculpture and photography. In doing so, the artist hopes to raise questions about the cultural place of books as a repository of knowledge and the future of the book in an increasingly digital age.

1 **Carmen.** Houston *Yellow Pages* phone book, 2007.
2 (Top to bottom) **Anthology.** *Norton Anthology of Masterpieces (7th Edition)* paperback, 2004; **Secret.** Torn pages from paperback books *Frankenstein* and *Dracula*, 2007; **Whirligig.** Paperback book, 2006.

2

1

2

3

Ferry Staverman

The Netherlands

Since 2000, Dutch artist Ferry Staverman has been making objects based on drawings using white or painted cardboard. Cardboard serves as a suitable and cheap material for Staverman's artistic experimentation. Staverman's first paper objects were small in size, ranging between 30 to 40 centimetres high; today, he makes objects between 60 to 80 centimetres high. For exhibitions, some paper objects grow to a height of 3.5 metres.

The shapes of Staverman's objects suggest movement, a dance or a fountain. The shapes are made with a sawing machine and built up in layers. After the back layer is removed, the object is "blown out" to form a three-dimensional object. Wires are used to hold the different layers in place, while also adding a geometric pattern to the object. The light around the sculptures makes the shapes "move" and "reflect".

4

1 **Red Spout.** Cardboard, wire and paint, 2006.
2 **Yellow Spout.** Cardboard, wire and paint, 2006.
3 **Green Stupa with Seven Hearts.** Cardboard, wire and paint, 2007.
4 **Yellow Stupa with Seven Hearts.** Cardboard, wire and paint, 2007.
5 **Head of the Artist.** Cardboard, paint and wire, 2006.

5

1

2

Jen Stark

United States

Jen Stark's work is a trip into technicolour paper splendour. The Fine Arts graduate from the Maryland Institute of Art began experimenting with paper on a student exchange to France, where she got her hands messy with the cheapest material available. Inspired by the unseen potential of common things, the forms of Stark's paper works are inspired by mysteries – those found at the bottom of the ocean or at the edge of the universe. Using ideas of replication and infinity on a minute scale, Stark repeats patterns and intelligent designs found in nature with layers of coloured paper constructions to form exuberant graphic images of paper eruptions, swirls, and curves.

1 **Tranfixed.** Cardstock paper, 2008.
2 **Candy Land.** Cardstock paper, 2008.

3 Over and Out. Coloured paper, 2008.

1

Schleeh Design
Canada

Trained in furniture design in Stuttgart and cabinet making in Canada, internationally-recognised Canadian artist Colin Schleeh started Schleeh Design in 2000 as demand grew for his one-of-a-kind furniture, accessories and sculptural art pieces. Today, a 7000-square-foot design and manufacturing studio by the Lachine Canal in Montreal produces the handmade products designed by Schleeh.

His award-winning desktop series of paper notepads twisted sculptures. "I love giving a "common material regal context, through thoughtful and innocent admiration, by studying its absolute, rather than its commonly valued properties," says Schleeh. Schleeh's designs ingeniously balance form and function, providing a compelling example of functional art.

1 **Wave.** Envirographic 100% recycled paper, 2008.
2 **Morph pad.** Envirographic 100% recycled paper, 2004.

2

3

4

5

3 **Wedge**. Envirographic 100% recycled paper, 2008.
4 **Mighty Morph Pad – Multi Stripe**. Envirographic 100% recycled paper, 2004.
5 **Erosion**. Envirographic 100% recycled paper, 2008.

1

Ingrid Siliakus
The Netherlands

Dutch artist Ingrid Siliakus' was initiated into paper architecture by discovering Japanese Professor Masahiro Chatani's work in the 1980s. Struck by the beauty and ingenious workings of his paper pieces, Siliakus studied Chatani's designs for several years before designing buildings by master architects such as Hendrik Petrus Berlage and Antoni Gaudi. Siliakus' expertise at making intricate paper constructions of buildings was picked up by the Museum of Modern Art (MoMA) in New York. She was invited to design an invitation card for the new MoMA building in 2004; these cards were produced and sold in MoMA's design shops.

After several years of making designs of existing buildings, Siliakus took a cue from M.C. Escher, a Dutch graphic artist known for his "impossible" constructions in woodcuts, lithographs and mezzotints, and began designing abstract paper sculptures. In 2005, she applied to exhibit at the Holland Paper Biennial 2006 and progressed from making one-sided art works to multiple-sided sculptures. This resulted in a series of sculptures embedded in folders, rather like pop-up books. These collections include *Stairs-mapping*, *Parallel Reflections*, *Windows to Balcony* and *Escalator*. These books can be opened up in various extents to display varying geometric formations; some of the books can open up 360 degrees.

1 **Parallel Reflections.** 160-225gsm paper, 2007.
2 **Reflections on Sangrada Familia.** 250gsm Rives Artist paper and 200gsm Rives Artist paper, 2008.

2

3

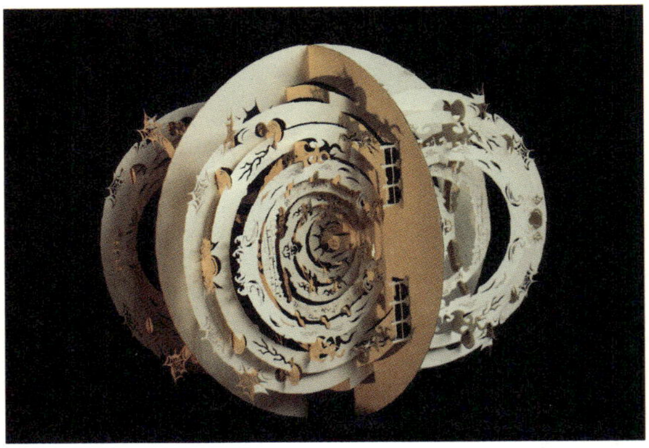

4

You discovered paper architecture through the work of Professor Masahiro Chatani. How did you proceed from there?
All the books by Professor Masahiro Chatani I could get my hands on were mostly in Japanese. Since I do not understand Japanese, I had to rely on the patterns in the books. I learned the technique of paper architecture by just studying these patterns: calculating the spaces between the cutting and folding lines to grasp the basics. When I finally understood the basics, I started to first make simple one-layered designs before progressing to making multiple-layered designs.

What is involved in the calculation of the spaces between the folds and cuts?
Mathematics is at the very core of creating a paper architecture piece. Without mathematics, there is no paper architecture. The proportions between the folding lines of a design must be calculated up to a hundredth of a millimetre. If this is not done correctly, I will immediately notice this in an artwork. The fold lines yield and have the tendency to break when not calculated correctly.

How long does the process of designing a pattern take?
Making designs involves calculating over and over again, next to drawing the layers of the object. Designing a paper architecture pattern is an extensive process that can take up to several weeks and more and lead to 30 or more prototypes. Each prototype needs to be cut, folded and examined before I can progress to next prototype.

It must have been a difficult leap to make from following Professor Chatani's patterns to making your own designs.
I discovered that I needed to visualise the object in three-dimensional form. In my view, it is impossible to design a paper architecture pattern without seeing an object like this in one's mind. It was a slow and difficult process to adjust to thinking three-dimensionally. Maybe it sounds strange but it feels like a reservoir opens up in my mind when I switch from thinking two-dimensionally to three-dimensionally. When this reservoir opens, it allows me to see things spatially in my mind's eye.

Besides learning to visualise and calculate the designs for a pattern, paper itself has its own unique qualities. What did you learn about your medium?
Paper has a mind of its own which asks for cooperation rather than manipulation. It is interesting to seek this cooperation with each separate paper brand. I usually work with paper between 160 and 300 grammes. I like to use 160 grammes best, since this paper weight is easy to fold, although it always depends on how well the fold lines are cut.

What do you use for larger sculptures?
With large sculptures, 160 grammes will not do, since the sculpture gets too weak, so I use heavier paper between 225 and 300 grammes.

Are the different types of paper tested for their suitability?
Not all paper is suitable for cutting or folding, so this needs to be tested with each paper brand. You also have to consider whether a certain paper brand will colourise over time. Right now I like to work with the paper brand Arches (France), which has a very subtle structure, and Rives Artist (France). Rives Artist is often used for (art) books. The sizes of my work vary from something 10 to 15 centimetres to a maximum of 60 by 30 by 30 centimetres.

How do people respond to your work?
People that see my artworks are intrigued and curious. They have a hard time understanding that a simple, let alone complicated, object can be created out of just pieces of paper. The technique of paper architecture is fairly new in the Western world. For many people, this is the first time they see work created with this technique.
They don't believe that it is possible.

Do you demonstrate the process for them?
People like to see a piece folded flat again to truly believe it is possible. At some exhibitions, I provide simple unfolded cards that people can fold themselves to have a better understanding of the technique. Besides the fact that the technique of paper architecture is not well-known in the West, the technique of creating multiple-sided, complicated and detailed sculptures is also unique.

5

3 Windows to Balcony. 160-225gsm paper, 2008.
4 Innerrings. 300gsm Ostrich paper and 290gsm papyrus paper, 2006.
5 Stairsmapping. 160-225gsm paper, 2007.

6

6 Escalator. 160-225gsm paper, 2008.

Interiors & Installations

What is the holy grail of paper?

At Canadian firm molo, the designers dream of "a water-resistant, fire-resistant, tear-resistant, recyclable, light-weight, economical paper created in an environmentally-sustainable way". Product designers around the world are experimenting with alternative materials and manufacturing methods, with paper entering the spotlight for its availability, potential for recycling and versatility. Artists too are exploring the physical and emotional properties of paper to reshape spatial environments through installations in innovative retail and exhibition concepts. These paper works inhabit the unlikely space of embodying both the functions of design and the conceptual premises of art, possessing beauty and usability.

In *Interiors & Installations*, paper leaves its role as a two-dimensional material to reveal its potential as a material for building furniture, products and spatial installations. *Interiors & Installations* showcases a stimulating range of furniture, interior products and installations where paper is being applied in unexpected ways. The designs in *Interiors & Installations* reveal an attention to material craft, processes of making, and conceptual thinking. From paper vessels being used to carry water and furniture made from shredded office documents, to building a paper crane as a way of launching a washing machine and abstract paper installations forming the backdrop of a retail store, *Interiors & Installations* showcases how designers and artists are creating new uses and fresh relevance for paper.

softseating. Brown kraft paper (50% recycled content), 2006. By molo.

1

Jo Meesters
The Netherlands

Studio Jo Meesters creates concepts and products based on the key words of matter and craftsmanship. The studio's practice operates as a laboratory for product concepts, researching new and innovative materials and techniques while exploring the boundaries of the intersection of craftsmanship and mass production techniques. *Pulp* is a collection of paper vessels by the studio, helmed by Dutch product designer Jo Meesters. Made entirely out of paper pulp, these vessels are surprisingly waterproof, the result of Meester's research into new techniques of working with materials. 24 pieces were produced in the first batch.

2

1~2 **Pulp.** Paper waste, newspapers, epoxy resin, wood glue and polyurethane resin, 2007.

What inspired the Pulp collection?
After travelling for two weeks, I came home and to my surprise, I couldn't open the door. A huge pile of local newspapers and ads had been delivered to my house. I was really shocked at the amount of waste paper I received in a short time.

How did you develop the idea of waterproof paper vessels?
The idea of putting water into paper vessels somehow intrigued me. By combining other materials with paper pulp such as epoxy and polyurethane, a new material is born with its own characteristics, leading to a series of vessels made out of paper that can hold water. Also, it gave the material the right contrast: it became shiny and hard instead of soft and rough.

How long did it take to produce the Pulp collection?
For the first five months, I spent time finding out the right mixture to apply into the pulp and the best way to produce the vessels without destroying the vessels.

Why did you choose the colour black for the collection?
Black has a very classic and contemporary feel. The idea of "using dead materials" (materials that have ended up as waste) is similar to black: the waste which is dead and black is resurrected into new products.

1

1 **One Day Paper Waste – Table.** Shredded confidential documents, shredded *Elle Décor* magazines and resin, 2008. The second edition of the *One Day Paper Waste – Cabinet* concept.

2 Detail of shredded paper of *One Day Paper Waste* series.

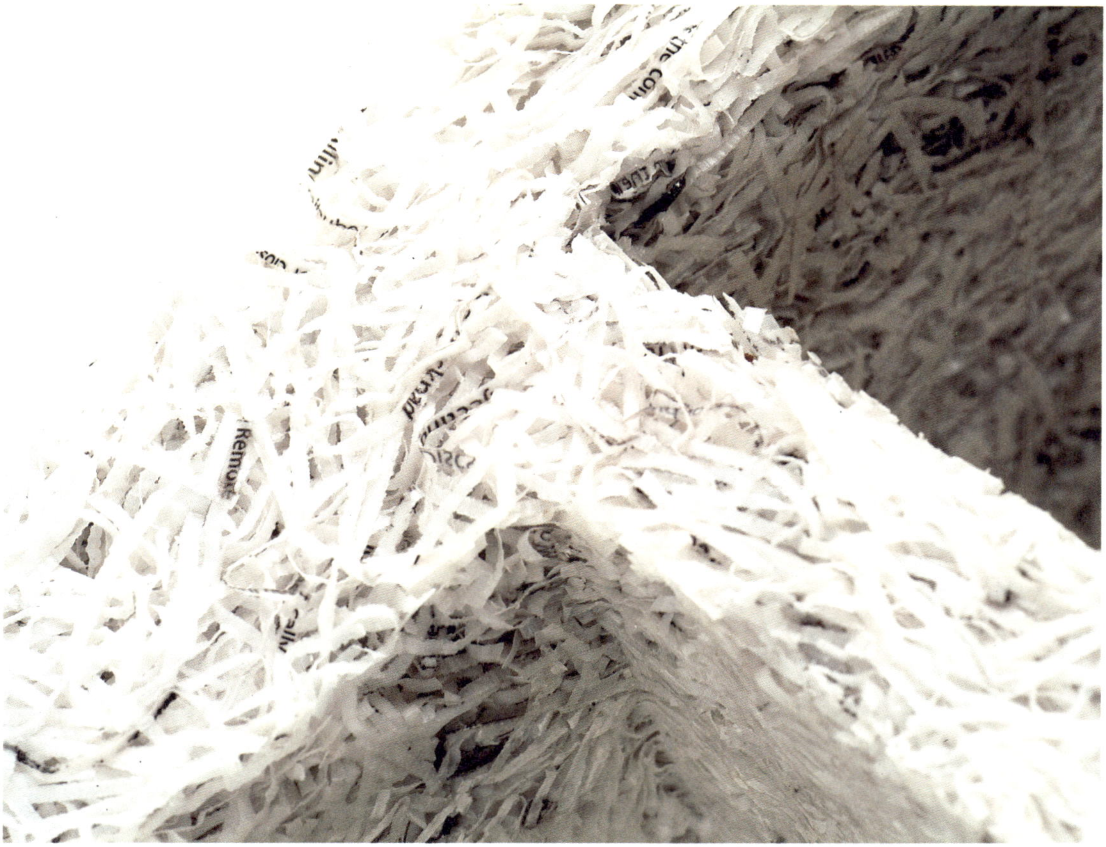

2

Jens Praet

Belgium

With a Masters in Conceptual Design in Context from the prestigious Design Academy Eindhoven, Belgian designer Jens Praet pursues a passion for materials and an interest in recycling through the objects he designs. The observation of unusual, tiny details and daily issues are often the starting point of his work. He exhibited the *One Day Paper Waste – Cabinet* at Droog Design's *Smart Deco 2* exhibition at the Salone del Mobile 2007. Taking shredded documents, Praet combined the shredded paper with resin and compressed them into a strong mould; the resulting material is a paper object as strong as wood.

Praet attributes the positive public response to *One Day Paper Waste* to the unique material and that "each piece of furniture is a one-off." Launching the *One Day Paper Waste – Table* at *EatDrinkDesign*'s exhibition at the Dutch Design Week 2007 in Eindhoven, the table is now being produced by Droog Design. According to Praet, a regular office produces enough shredded documents every day to make a piece of his paper furniture.

4

3 **Shredded Paper Storage**. Recycled shredded paper, resin with black pigments, 2008. Commissioned by L'Uomo Vogue, in collaboration with Yamamay, Praet designed this new black edition in line with the *One Day Paper Waste* family for the *Yamazonia – The Design and the Nature* event in Milan.

4 **One Day Paper Waste – Cabinet**. Shredded confidential documents and resin, 2007. Praet reacted to the problem of office waste by reusing shredded documents into a useful object with new dignity.

1

Publique Living

United States

"They're so cute" is the common response to the *PopMat Paper Placemats*, a series of dining placemats from San Francisco-based firm Publique Living. Illustrations are laser-cut from paper with the images "popped" up to give the everyday dining placemat graphic element. Since branching out to home accessories in early 2001, designer Lian Ng has been combining his expertise in graphic design and paper-based design to develop new products.

The idea for the *PopMats* started with die-cutting. The original illustrations made by Ng were too complicated for a conventional die. Laser-cutting was chosen to allow Ng to maintain the complex details in the illustration.

Each mat was cut individually to avoid back-burn. A laser beam was calibrated to maintain a kerf (width of the cut made by the laser beam) for inline details in the illustration and the resolution adjusted for smoothness in the curves. The speed and power of the laser was balanced for the least amount of edge-burn.

"Paper placemats exist and so do pop-up cards, but the combination of the two comes together and creates something new yet familiar," says Ng. The design also demonstrates Publique Living's interest in ecological design by exploring how far a design can go with reducing the dependency on the printing process to produce an image.

2

1~2 **PopMat Paper Placemats.** 100% recycled paper (30% post-consumer fibre and 70% pre-consumer waste paper), 2008. Placemats for a table setting in the form of pop-up graphics; each design incorporates an area to write the name of your guest, functioning also as a name card.

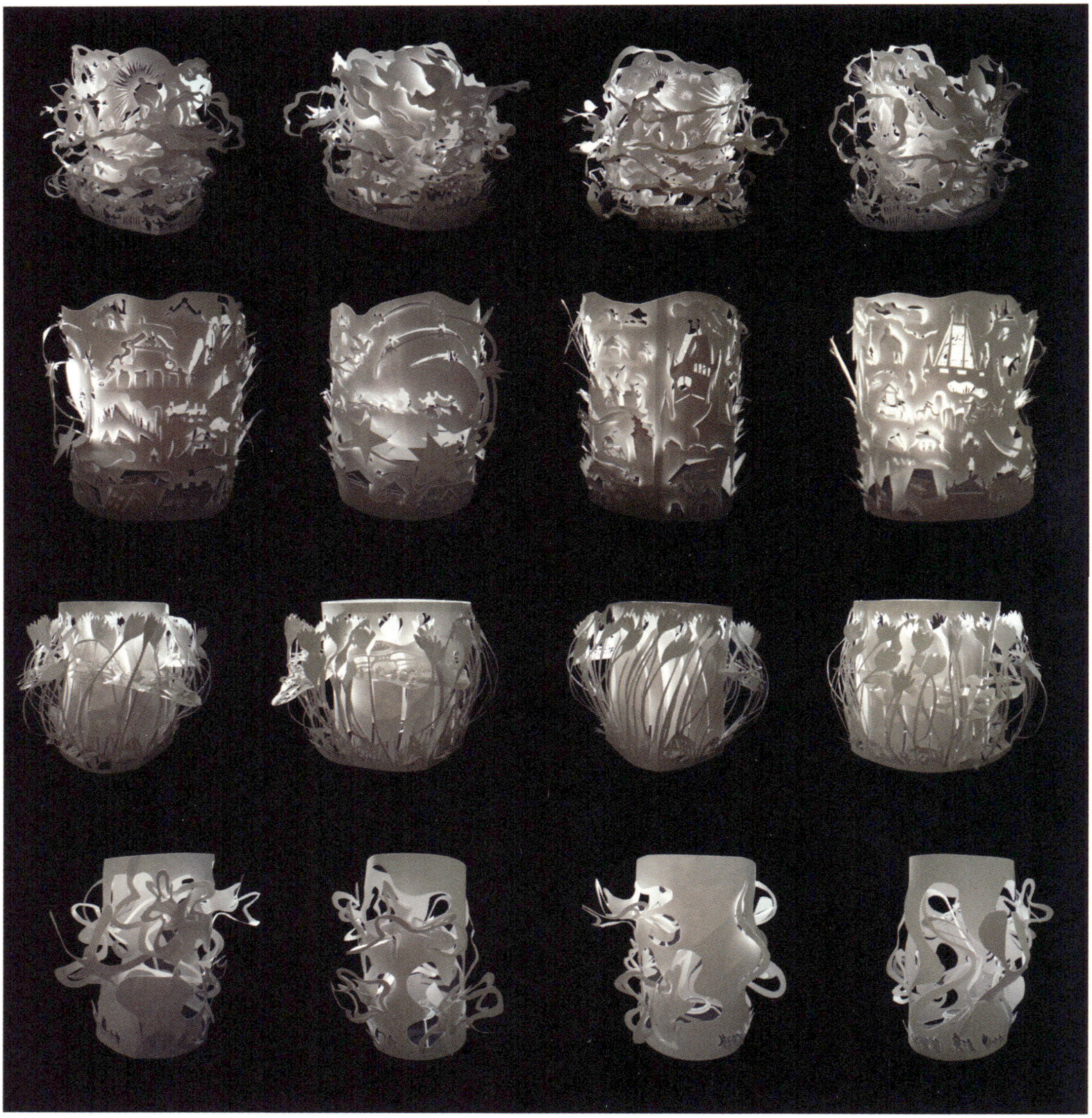

1

Yu Jordy Fu

United Kingdom

A senior architectural designer at Skidmore, Owings and Merrill and a former designer at Future Systems, Yu Jordy Fu's work pushes the boundaries between art, design and architecture. The *Cloud Lamp* shades are made out of recycled paper and is an expression of Fu's wish to create a sustainable future, tapping also into a cloud motif to evoke a soft, intimate atmosphere. The *Cloud Lamps* can be flat packed and are sold with a milky white energy-saving bulb.

1 **Cloud Lamp – Angels, Prague, Memories, Grandpa.** Recycled paper, 2008.

2 **Family.** Recycled paper, 2007.

2

3

3 Cloud Lamp – Complete series. Recycled paper, 2008.

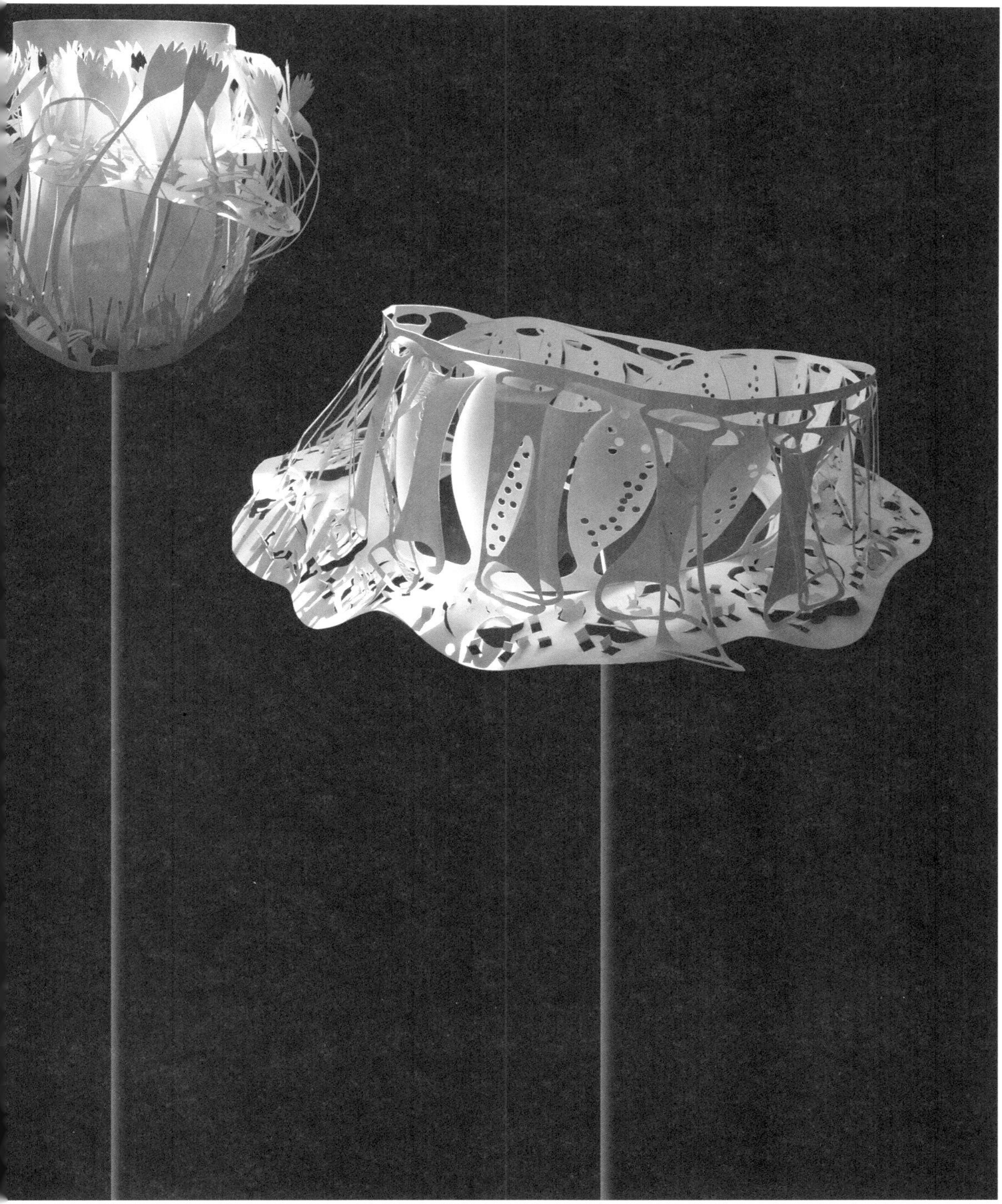

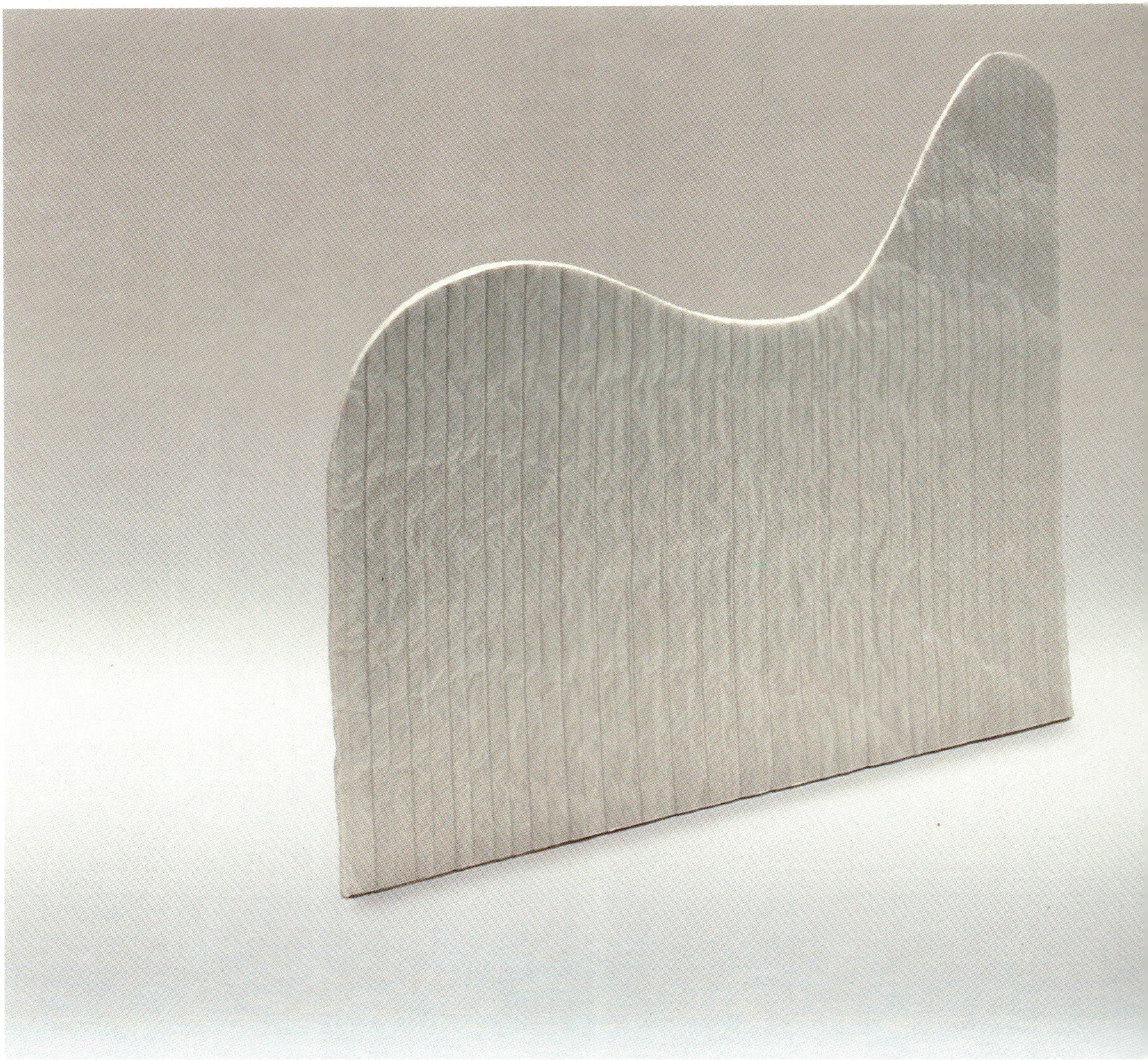

1

Tokujin Yoshioka Design

Japan

Selected as one of "100 Japanese Respected by the World" in the Japanese edition of *Newsweek*, Tokujin Yoshioka is celebrated for his innovative and subtle use of materials, creating objects, furnishings and installations that are regarded as much for their functionalism as their ethereal beauty. Some of Yoshioka's most famous works include the *Tokyo-pop Chair*, *Media Skin* for the au design project, the *Chair That Disappears in the Rain* made of special glass, and many projects for Issey Miyake including shop design and installation for A-POC and ISSEY MIYAKE.

One of Yoshioka's most famous works, the *Honey-pop Chair* is made with 120 sheets of glassine paper piled together and cut along specific lines so that it magically opens up into a honeycomb structure. The final form of the chair is set when it responds to the shape of the first sitter's bottom. The *Honey-pop Chair* is now a part of the permanent collection at the Museum of Modern Art (MoMA), Vitra Design Museum, the Centre Pompidou, and Victoria and Albert Museum.

1 Honey-Pop Chair. Glassine paper, 2001. .

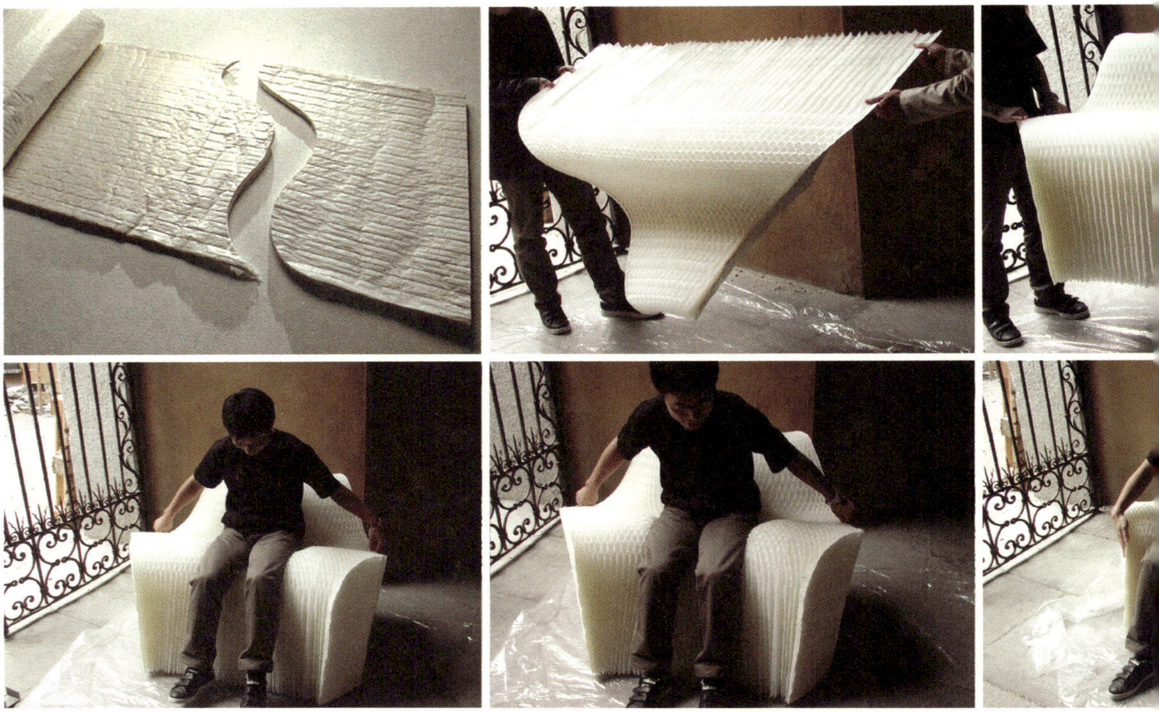

2

2 The two-dimensional design of the *Honey Pop Chair* opens up to reveal a honey-comb structure; its final shape conforms to the bottom of the first sitter.

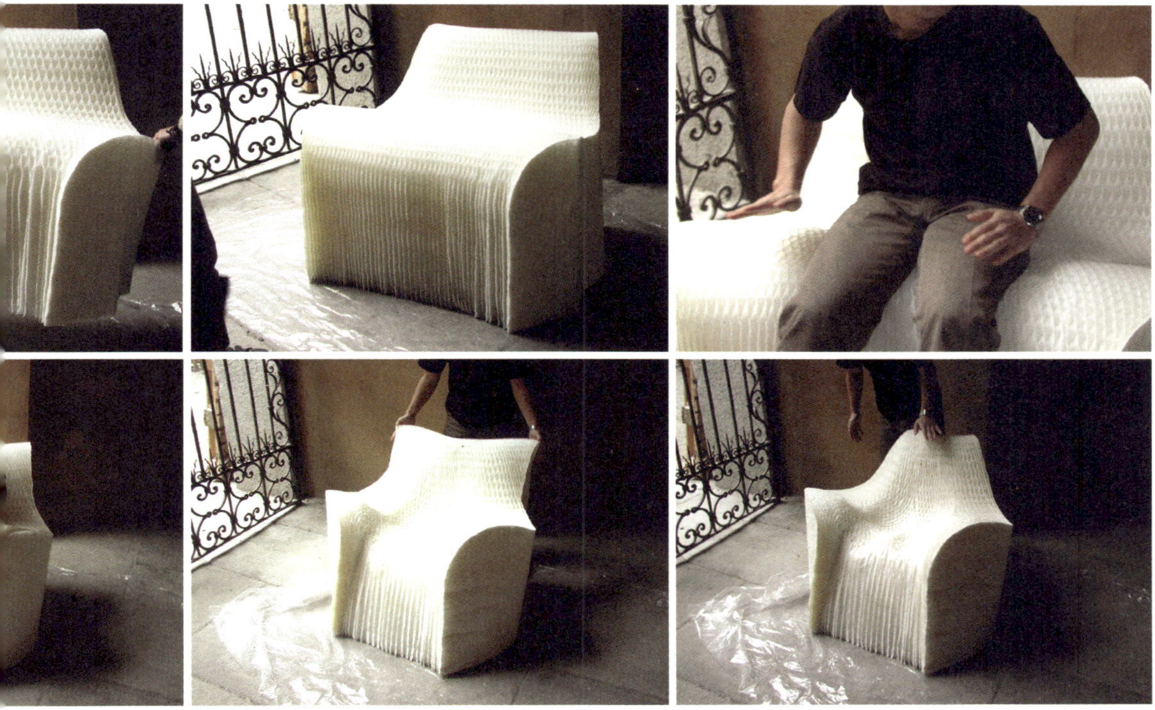

3

4

In collaboration with Moroso, Yoshioka covered the Moroso Showroom in New York with approximately 30,000 sheets of tissue. "I have always felt the beauty of this silk-like paper and am amazed [at] how the simple, ordinary material like tissue can remind me of a snow scape," says Yoshioka. His design intends to reach the law of nature, creating scenes which arise when enormous numbers of small transparent materials are organised and piled together, giving the material depth and density. Yoshioka's creates a new scenery through this installation of tissues which evokes one's emotions and remembrance.

3~5 **Moroso New York**. Tissue paper, 2007. An installation at the Moroso showroom in New York.

5

1

Matt Gagnon Studio

United States

"It is necessary for me as a designer to work in various mediums to stay interested in the process of making," says Matt Gagnon, who works out of his studio in New York's hipster Williamsburg neighbourhood, the current breeding ground for the city's creative class, "Each new project brings up new issues and new problems to learn from which can be incorporated into the next project".

Trained as an architect and a former design associate with Frank Gehry's design team, Gagnon has been pursuing an independent broad-based design practice since 2002. Aside from client-based work, he has been involving himself in conceptually-oriented, speculative research-driven projects that explore the nebulous and stimulating territory between art and design. "I think this notion of design and art being completely separate entities is a result of the industrial revolution and mass production," shares Gagnon, "I believe the creative process of both employ similar operations. The distinction is sometimes only a matter of context and, of course, intention." Made by hand out of Gagnon's studio, the *Papertable* and *Paper-sidetables* are a magazine-newspaper rack and coffee table-magazine rack respectively. Following a trip to Monument Valley at the southern border of the state of Utah, Gagnon came upon the idea of exploring "the idea of creating something solid that would also indicate the effects of time" in his products.

The abstract forms of the two products were also inspired by Monument Valley's desert landscape. "When you actually visit the place, you do not only see buttes and mesas but feel them due to their mass," comments Gagnon on the rock formations which emerged over thousands of years from the erosion of desert plateaus, "I wanted to make something that could be felt as well as seen. So I designed thepiece to have a some-what random appearance yet remain highly functional."

The resulting coffee table is made from layers of recycled paper board that have been laser cut and bolted together in the form of irregular rock formations. As for a final poetic effect, the paper registers use like a fine piece of leather, gaining character and meaning over time.

2

1 **Papertable.** Homasote (building material made from recycled newsprint) mechanical fasteners, linseed oil and acrylic adhesive, 2005.

2 Samples of studies done for the design of the *Papertable*.

Paper is hardly a sturdy material to be used for furniture. As an architect and designer, what is the potential for paper in product design?
I think paper with the proper treatment can be used in many situations not normally associated with paper. Ultimately, practical issues such as sustainability and durability play a role in choosing the right material for an application. But I can imagine more products or components from pressed or cast paper that would allow for easy recycling.

A number of designers are discovering, even inventing, their own methods of production. Your paper tables appear to be an example of this.
Yes. The actual form of the coffee table could have been made in various materials and produced using various techniques.But once we settled on an approach using laser-cut paper board, it suggested a range of designs which I think the side tables explores.

The side tables are made using a random selection and ordering of a certain number of uniquely shaped cut-outs. The result is that each table is slightly different without any extra work involved. Designing the process in addition to the form is what enables the design to be what it is.

What were your intentions for the design?
I started out wanting to design a piece that was "heavy," which for me was in response to the type of work that mass production and international shipping encourages – flat and lightweight. I was inspired by the mesas and buttes in the American Southwest. The different size cuts in the table accommodate different-sized reading materials. So as the table is used for storing magazines, newspapers and books, the cuts are filled in to recreate the solid block of paper.

In addition to the visual weight of the table, the paper also provided a literal softness to the touch. The outside surface is finished to have a suede or velvet-like quality. There is a surprise when someone touches the piece expecting it to be concrete.

How do the paper tables change over time?
One type of change results from the type and quantity of reading materials stored in the slots – whether the table is full or empty. A conceptual idea is that there is a dialogue between the raw material – magazines etc., and the finished product – recycled paper board; highlighting the potential life cycle of a material. The tables are simply one use for the recycled paper board.

The papertables also addresses the question of the life cycle of materials, how a material itself changes over time.
A more long term transition is that due to the relative softness of the tables, they will literally change over time with wear and develop a desirable patina similar to old wooden tables. For me this recalls the mesas, as those rock forms are a result of thousands of years of erosion.

3

3 **Papersidetable.** Homasote (building material made from recycled newsprint) mechanical fasteners, linseed oil and acrylic adhesive, 2006.

PUSH>

Germany

"If you don't like my work, make your own": this was the reply given to Robert Buss' when he suggested a colleague use just paper to make stools instead of both paper tubes and wood. Shortly after, his partner from PUSH>, Ute Conen, started to collect paper rolls left over from the plotters in her office. A collection of about 200 paper tubes joined the duo in an empty apartment in the former East Germany where they decided to build all of their furniture from paper tubes, including a shelving system inspired by Aldo Rossi, tables and stools. Some of the pieces were later borrowed by a paper maker for an exhibition, leading to an invitation to exhibit at the Max Planck Institute in Leipzig, Germany.

"We decided that the exhibit at the Max Planck Institute was a good chance to revisit our whole range of paper furniture and to generate a coherent exhibit," shares Buss. The Max Planck Institute became part of the inspiration for the *Disposable Office*. "The complex is very large with an internal 'street' connecting the different buildings that is supposed to function as a communication zone," adds Buss, "Unfortunately, this space has no furniture to facilitate communication."

Buss and Conen decide to create a range of disposable furniture with the concept of furniture for the information age with information in the form of recycled paper. The *Disposable Office* collection continues the work of PUSH>, a virtual company using global resources to produce innovative products. Buss and Conen have produced about 20 different designs for the collection so far, using glues recyclable with paper and no solvent or chemical-based coatings.

Buss attests to the durability of his paper furniture, "We have made a high chair for our first child which survived so well that the second child also used it". However, he has had to make the collection by hand due to a lack of manufacturing methods to produce the paper furniture He adds, "Paper furniture can be more expensive than IKEA furniture because the production system isn't behind it."

1

1 **Disposable Office.** Paper tubes from recycled paper, tempered glass, 2004.

2

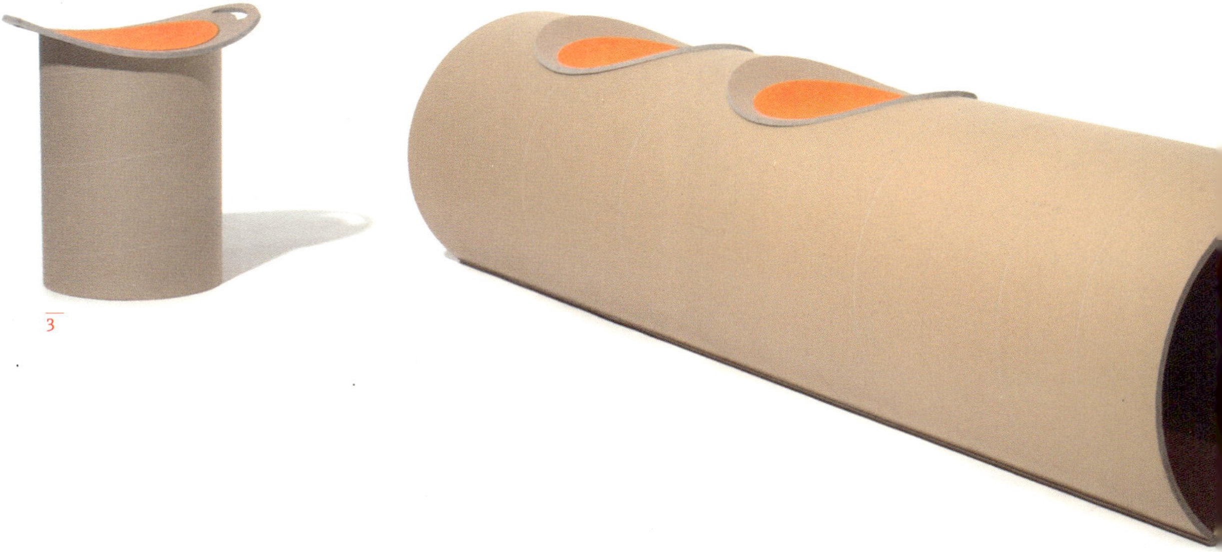

3

2~4 **Disposable Office.** Paper tubes from recycled paper, tempered glass, 2004.

How were the pieces of furniture in Disposable Office constructed?
The furniture has been constructed by hand using a simple fixtures, presses and clamps. The tubes get sawed to length and glued into sub-modules. These modules are glued together to for pieces. Surfaces are laminated and then glued onto the assembled structure.

What type of paper was used to make the Disposable Office collection?
For the finished pieces, the paper is a standard recycled brown paper consisting of over 97 per cent recycled material, which we sourced from a regional supplier of paper tubes (Pappröhren Wolfgang Müller). In a furniture series, it is important to have a consistent colour, wrapping angle, wrapping gap and diameter. These factors are not consistent in the paper rolls that we collected from plotters. We were also able to use thinner walled rolls than what we often find from the plotter, thus creating lighter furniture.

What was the rationale for using tubes as the "structure" for the design?
The reason for using the tubes is mostly aesthetic. We find that the repetitive structure with clean edges is preferable to many other methods of constructing paper furniture. The pieces are also durable; the majority of our chairs look almost like new.

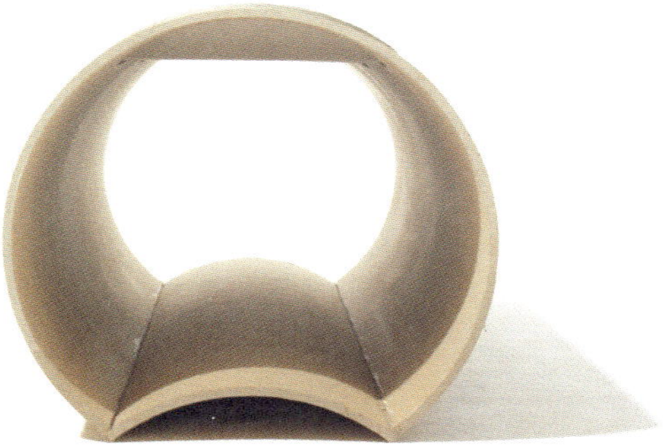

4

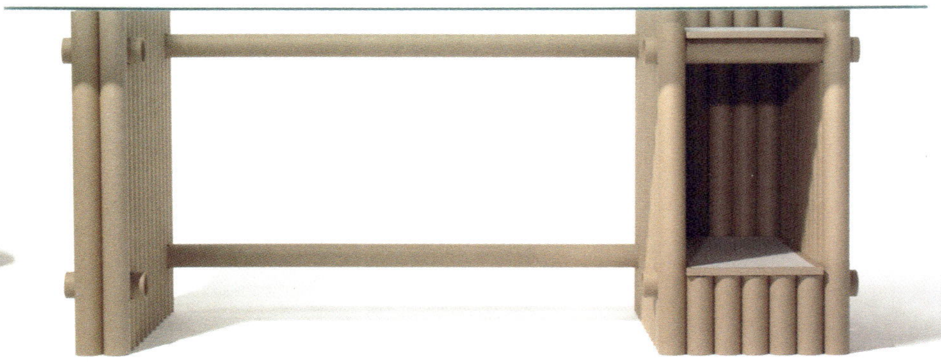

1

Nendo
Japan

What is the 21st century man? How should he work, live and play? In the *XXIst Century Man* exhibition held at 21_21 Design Sight in Tokyo – a destination offering perspectives on the world through design – curator and fashion maverick Issey Miyake asked Oki Sato, the founder of Japanese design firm Nendo, to design a chair out of pleated paper, a waste product produced in mass amounts during the process of making pleated fabric. The task was to consider how contemporary individuals can create a better future through the search for new images, new products and new sensibilities which could address the issues facing the 21st century individual.

"Our solution to his challenge transformed a roll of pleated paper into a small chair that appears naturally as you peel away its outside layers, one layer at a time," states Sato. When Sato presented his design to Miyake, Miyake responded by saying the chair looked like a cabbage – and the *Cabbage Chair* was born. In order to "peel' open the chair, the user has to take a scissors to cut open the layers, revealing a poetic design of a chair with no internal structure and is, ultimately, unfinished. "Customers can make it any height and width as they want, which is very interesting for us," comments Sato.

The *Cabbage Chair* fulfils the cherished goals of being cost-effective because of the pleated paper material as well as being aesthetically pleasing, soft, and comfortable, a design worthy of a company named one of "The Top 100 Small Global Companies" by *Newsweek* in 2007.

1 Cabbage Chair. Pleated paper, 2008. Resins were added during the original paper production, adding strength and making the paper able to remember forms; the pleats give the chair elasticity and a springy resilience.

2

3

2~3 The *Cabbage Chair* can be shipped as a compact roll for the user to cut open and peel at home.

4

4 **Cabbage Chair.** Pleated paper, 2008.

1

molo
Canada

molo is a Vancouver-based design studio, dedicated to materials research and an exploration of space-making. In 2003, architects Stephanie Forsythe and Todd MacAllen partnered with long-time friend Robert Pasut to form molo. In 2008, there were 18 people working across a variety of roles from design and architecture, materials research and product development to graphic design, business administration and manufacturing. A genuinely collaborative open studio, molo creates and distributes innovative products to clients around the world.

"We start simply by designing for ourselves and inspiration comes through a hands-on process and curiosity for understanding materials, structure and the world we experience around us," says Forsythe. The design of molo's products are an outgrowth of Forsythe and MacAllen's architectural explorations. The duo are inspired by the intimate and tactile experience that the smaller scale of furniture has in architecture. Hands-on making and the primary functions of touch and sound are fundamental to their education as architects and as designers.

softseating is a collection of seating which uses a honeycomb structure to fan open into stools, benches, and loungers. Magnetic end panels allow an element to connect to itself, forming a cylindrical stool or low table, or to connect to other elements of the same size in the series, forming winding benches and endless possibilities for seating topographies. The beauty of these pieces comes from their sculptural abstract forms. The seating is available in natural, unbleached brown kraft paper and kraft paper which

2

has been dyed a deep black with bamboo charcoal ink to emphasise the geometric pattern of light and shadow in the honeycomb structure. Materials used are 100 per cent recyclable, and are not intended to be disposable – the paper gets better with age. With use, the edges of the paper gently soften and crush, creating irregular facets forming a unique organic pattern within the crisp honeycomb geometry.

1~2 softseating. Brown kraft paper (50% recycled content), 2006.

3

Forsythe and MacAllen are trained as architects, but have begun working increasingly in molo in product design. Why?
If you look at any city, it is the largely the systems of construction which define the built environment. We believe in putting our energy and time into creating systems for construction. The furniture scale is part of this vision. It is a modest and natural place to have begun to grow molo's production abilities and full-scale experiments. It has also always been interesting for us to work on a variety of scales; this is connected from the perspective of how people experience their environments.

In the last five years, we have focused on building a way of working. We have been designing a business model that will sustain ongoing creative exploration. We see the work we have been doing with paper and textile honeycomb structures as just the beginning of a lifetime's worth of research, development and experimentation into the potential for structural space-making systems that can make very efficient use of material and embody beautiful sculptural form and flexibility.

In molo's unique practice, you bring together the sensibilities and concerns of architecture, material craft and design.
Working at a furniture scale, directly with materials, heightens our sense for the human scale and physical experience in architecture. Conversely, product and furniture design benefits from the perspective of thinking in the larger context of place and space making. For example, the paper seating

4

we have designed is about the space you can create with a topography of seating and not about a chair as a finite object. There is not a singular form that any of our seating is intended to take; they are designed to be shaped to a temporal situation or a given space.

Did you find paper a suitable material to work with?
Paper is visually delicate, yet surprisingly strong when you pay attention to the direction of the grain of the paper. We orient the grain of the paper to align with the direction of the honeycomb cells, thus creating a very strong, lightweight structure in our paper *softwalls* and *softseating*.

Paper has actually been an easy material to work with; it laminates and works with the machines well. It was also easy to find non-toxic glues to work with paper which will not yellow in sunlight. Salt-based fire retardants work well with paper because it is absorbent. Paper is one of the most readily recycled materials in the world and so it is easy to source recycled content. The big challenge is water.

How do the qualities of paper work with your products?
One of the most impressive things about *paper softwalls* is the way a little bit of material can go a long way. A softwall that can open to over six metres in length consists of mostly air, and can compress to less than four centimetres – the thickness of a book – for storage and shipping.

Despite being made from simple lightweight sheets of humble materials such as paper and non-woven textiles, the honeycomb geometry lends these structures great strength and flexible resilience, with an economy of material resource.

We are also very fond of the way paper ages and have been delighted to find so many other people enjoy this aspect of our *paper softseating*.

molo works with factories to produce and prefabricate your products. How highly is the company involved in the manufacturing process?
We have a very close relationship with the manufacturers. This has been one of the core intentions in setting up molo as a way of working, to be close to the making of things. When you are part of the process of making, you see opportunities for design improvisation along the way, how the process or the design might be improved or a new possibility entirely.

In another interview, MacAllen describes the goal of molo as "becoming your own clients to fund your own experiments and projects". How do you function as your own clients?
Our work is very intuitive; we pay attention to our senses and follow our curiosity. For us, it only makes sense to work very directly and not have a client between us and the things we are experimenting with and creating. We also see our design process as a body of open-ended research that we would not want to tie to any client's timeline, objectives or budget. We almost never start with the pre-determined end of a particular functional thing in mind, and if we do, it usually leads us in another direction anyway. We want to be open to discoveries in the process. We look for happy accidents.

3~4 **softblock**. Black kraft paper (50% recycled content), 2006. A modular system of building blocks to be stacked, joined or used on their own to create textured walls, or functional surfaces of varying heights and forms such as partitions, tables and bars.

5

6

5 **paper softwall.** Lightweight paper (black), 2004.
6 **Kraft paper softwall.** Brown kraft paper, 2007.

softwall belongs to molo's innovative and award-winning family of expandable-compressible honeycomb structures called *soft*. *softwall* was conceived by the desire for flexible and spontaneous space making, for the ability to shape more intimate, ephemeral space within larger open spaces in a temporal way, and then give that space back to the larger room when needed. Recognised for its poetic and pragmatic beauty and innovation, *softwall* has been acquired by the MOMA in New York City for its permanent collection. From its debut as a 1.8-metre-tall white paper wall, *softwall* has evolved into a full array materials, colours, and sizes to suit differing situations and requirements. *softwall* is available in two paper versions. *paper softwall*, with its hundreds of layers of light-weight tissue paper, has a delicate and ethereal beauty; the *kraft paper softwall*, constructed of an unbleached heavy kraft paper, has a weightier stiffness and warm earthy presence.

1

Mia Pearlman

United States

Mia Pearlman makes site specific paper-cut installations, ephemeral drawings which inhabit space in both two and three dimensions. "My work is meditation on chance, control and the ephemeral nature of reality. It is a reaction to the overwhelming knowledge we now have of every aspect of our world," says Pearlman. The works "evoke environmental chaos, physical instability, and infinite destructive forces beyond our control". Pearlman makes complex line drawings on large rolls of paper using India ink. The selected areas are cut out to make new drawing and pinned into a sculptural form to create a drawing in space.

1~2 **Maelstorm**. Basic drawing paper, aluminum, steel, paper, India ink, wire and monofilament, 2008. A giant multilevel mobile, 12-ft in diameter and 11-ft-high, with six independently rotating layers of cut paper, the work echoes the East river currents, cloud formations and the remainder of the nearby 9/11 skyline.

2

3

3 **Eddy**. Basic drawing paper, India ink, paperclips, tacks and monofilament, 2008. Pearlman used the same paper pieces as *Nigh* in a much smaller, more intimate space.

4 **Nigh**. Basic drawing paper, India ink, paperclips and tacks, 2007. The work envelops the viewer in its imaginary weather system.

4

1

Jum Nakao
Brazil

Brazilian designer Jum Nakao helped design the *Eggo*, an egg-shaped washing machine engineered to handle delicates for household appliances brand Brastemp. For the product's launch in Sao Paulo, Nakao came up with something special, imagining a big stork bringing the products to a baby, reminding the audience of birth and the purity.

A larger-than-life paper stork was made out of a 1000 pieces of paper and given life: Naná Lavander and Agustina Comas helped mechanise the bird to simulate flight while artist Paolo Beto recreated the sounds of the womb to further Nakao's idea of birth. An *Eggo* washing machine hangs from its mouth, much like the ancient stories of storks delivering babies to an expectant couple.

1–2 Eggo. White vegetable paper, 2007.

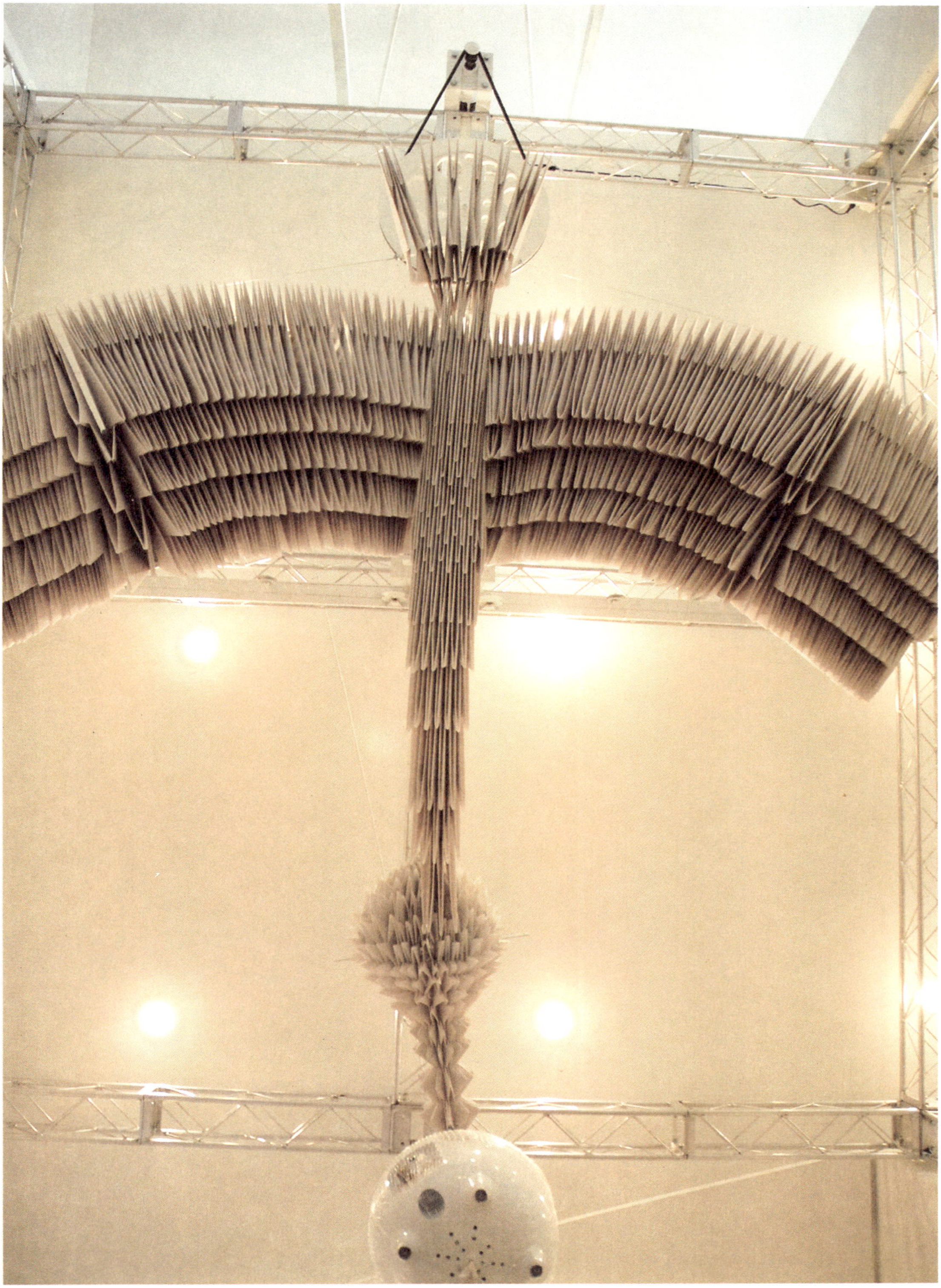

2

1

Katie Kulper

United States

A graphic design graduate from Portland State University, Katie Kulper constructed a springtime storefront installation for eco-friendly clothing and homewares boutique Olio United in Southeast Portland, USA. 1000 white and blue airplanes folded from recycled paper are suspended into an organic, wing-like formation at the window.

1 **Aircraft.** 100% recycled lined binder paper and recycled blue paper, thread and wire, 2008.

1

Maslen & Mehra

Australia

Two Australian artists working out of London, Tim Maslen and Jennifer Mehra's collaborative practice explores ideas revolving around the meeting point and overlapping of nature and culture. In *Gorge*, the artists aim to transform the gallery space into a fictitious landscape, using stacks of recycled books to evoke eroded rock contours jutting out of the gallery floor. The reference to nature is seen in the fragile plant forms which are cast in resin peeking out of the open book pages. The duo have exhibited widely including solo exhibitions in London, Sydney, New York, Paris, Istanbul, Barcelona, Rome and Berlin.

1~2 **Gorge.** Recycled books, wax, cast resin plant sculptures and cast rubber root sculptures, 2000.

2

dARCHstudio

Greece

Founded by architect and designer Elina Drossou in 2006, dARCHstudio's projects range from office buildings, residences, retail shops, ephemeral constructions and theoretical installations to small-scale projects like furniture, graphic design and set design. The renovation of the showroom YESHOP IN HOUSE, together with fashion designer, Yiorgos Eleftheriades, saw a 90-square-metre retail space in the centre of Psirri, Athens, being installed with a biomorphic wall construction made out of corrugated carton.

"The need to synthesise the two different approaches to design (fashion design and architecture) was the focal point of the project," states Drossou, "Concepts and practices used in fashion design were incorporated as organisational principles." 1500 sheets of corrugated carton made from 100 per cent recycled material were used for the site-specific construction, emphasising the dynamic properties of the space as well as fulfilling the client's wish to give the shop an ephemeral character.

For 15 days, a team constructed the fluid curves of the installation using 2000 blueprints showing the horizontal sections of the curved parts of the wall. Each hand-cut sheet of five-millimetres-thick carton was glued to its specific place, with the corrugated side of the carton exposed.

Existing furniture was rearranged and 'fitted' as if they had been were wedged into the cardboard. Boxes used as displays for the store's products were also worked into the installation. The displays are intensified with the use of built-in indirect lighting. The installation's abstract and fluid design resembles a living organism, producing a dynamic space which allows for varying views depending on one's position in the store.

1

1 **Papercut.** 1500 sheets of 5mm-thick corrugated carton and wood glue, 2007.

2

2 Each sheet of corrugated cardboard was cut and glued into place at the store.

3 Blueprints of the horizontal sections of the curved parts were produced for the installation.

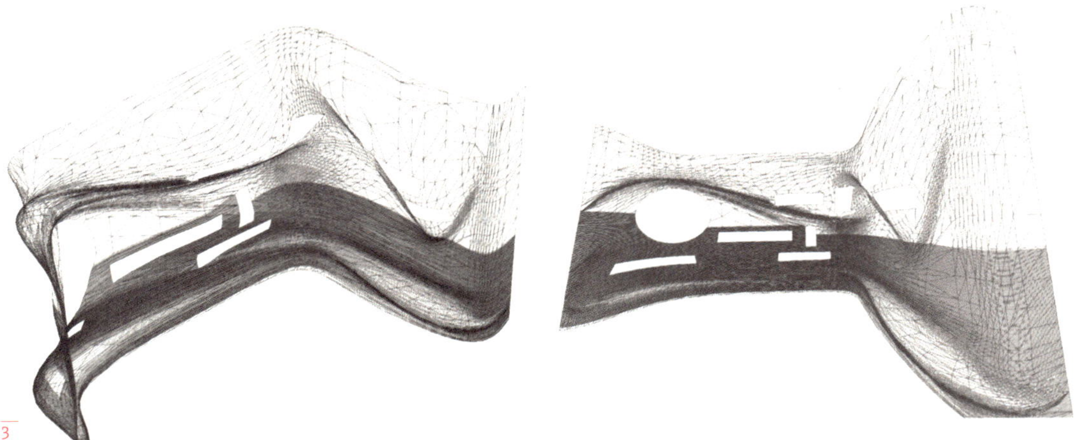

3

1

Andrea Dezsö

United States & Romania

Born and raised in Romania and ethnically Hungarian, Andrea Dezsö's work explores the realm of the deeply personal to the historic, psychological and social realms, reflecting her experience of growing up under Soviet-style communism. Based in New York today, she makes drawings, artist's books, multi-layered paper-cuts and installations; her work has been reviewed in *The New York Times* and *The Village Voice*.

"The common thread running through all my work is the aim to create an experience of beauty infused with mystery that we all knew well in childhood but rarely connect with during our adult lives," says Dezsö. In *Shadow Books* and *The Day We Changed Our Lives Forever*, Dezsö creates three layers of paper-cuts in a tunnel book. Fantastical characters and backdrops inhabit each frame, where the artist uses changing coloured lighting – from red to blue to green – to shift the mood and to tell an open-ended narrative.

1 **The Day We Changed Our Lives Forver.** Arches and Fabriano 100% rag paper, 2005. Interactive installation using hand-cut tunnel books.

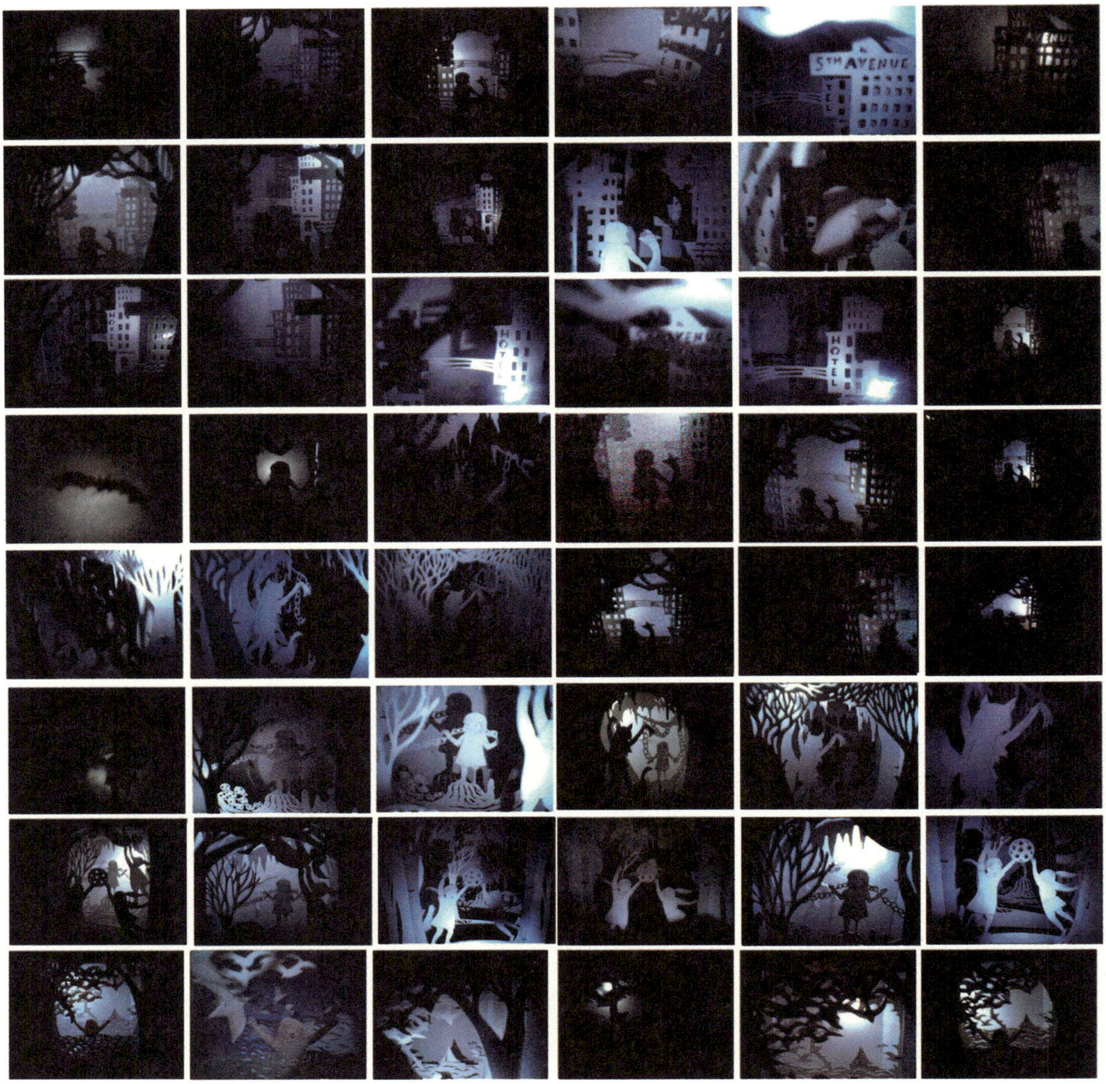

2

2 **Shadow Books.** Arches and Fabriano 100% rag paper, 2004. Interactive installation using hand-cut tunnel books illuminated with red, green and blue LED light. This project was exhibited at Flux Factory's Cartunnel Comix Fluxture show.

3 **Devil's Cave.** Arches and Fabriano 100% rag paper, 2005.

3

1

Sounds of Silence

Germany

Sounds of Silence is a collaboration between Frankfurt-based architect Petra Eichler and artist-director Susanne Kessler. Their work since their first collaboration in 2005 includes installations, objects and ambient environments, creating atmospheres that can be experienced and which invite the audience to be part of it.

Sounds of Silence's first project by the same name in 2005 is a series of installations on the different qualities of silence. Vacant properties in the city centre of Frankfurt including the hollowed structure of a former cinema, a former café, an enormous basement and "the whole world" were fitted with a series of audio-visual installations. Each installation creates an experience of a quality of silence as conceived by the artists.

The first installation, *sound 01*, in October 2005, works with the idea of "the kind of silence people only dream of". Inside a vacant building, 11 paper silhouettes measuring four metres by six metres were cut out from rolls of Tyvek. The cut-outs were separated into individual panes showing a slice of a forest. Each pane was suspended along a seven-metre-long framed structure to form the scene of a poetic forest clearing. The installation was accompanied by fluorescent tubes with alternating colours creating varying moods and a sound collage of isolated bird calls. A new version of *sound 01* was made for Droog Design at the Milan Furniture Fair in April 2006.

1~2 Sounds of Silence Sound 01. Tyvek, 2005.

Red Revisited
by Bas Warmoeskerken
Paradise Picnic
by Joost Grootens

1

25
200
300
300
300
71
71
422,5cm
625,0cm

2

3

3 The paper-cuts are layered to form a scene of a forest clearing.

4

The concept of a paper forest installation for the *Sounds of Silence sound 01* was translated onto a smaller scale for the vitrines of Van Cleef & Arpel's flagship store in Paris Place Vendôme. The outdoor vitrines were filled with motifs inspired by Van Cleef's elaborate jewellery and traditional Christmas tree decoration. A forest landscape forms the narrative stage for the jewellery with a fairytale atmosphere reminiscent a Walt Disney movie.

The two big vitrines inside the boutique were filled with a paper snowstorm and a magic deer scenery. All the paper works include a horizon-like background for a winter-like atmosphere. The lighting designer Gregor Knueppel used LED panels with programmed light sequences to accentuate the silhouettes of the paper-cuts while Sound Designer Martin Bott enhanced the sonic atmosphere with compositions of bells, the sound of snow blowing and whispering.

4~5 **Window Installation for Van Cleef & Arpels.** Tyvek (by Dupont), 2007. An installation for the Christmas season of 2007/2008.

5

Papering the Body

If you wear that paper dress.

Paper dresses were the rage in the United States in the 1960s – cheap, disposable items which came in a dazzling array of colourful Pop prints. Sold in flat packages in departmental stores, disposable paper dresses disappeared off the face of popular culture in a few years. Paper fashion items continued to make sporadic appearances. In 1995, Icelandic songstress Bjork appeared on the cover of her album, Post, in a paper Tyvek jacket by British-Turkish designer Hussein Chalayan. Paper occasionally graced the catwalks of high-street fashion – from Tao Kurihara's Spring/Summer 2007 collection to Helmut Lang's 1990 Paper Dress to fashion maverick Issey Miyake's Kamiko dress in the early 1980s.

Papering the Body showcases the exciting use of paper in crafted fashion items by contemporary designers and artists. Be it jewellery, dresses, masks or bodily accessories, *Papering the Body* celebrates the beautiful forms – bold and sculptural, light and ethereal – brought to life through paper. From paper dresses made from maps, to crumpled dresses with ghostly forms, to paper assembled into necklaces and earrings, or paper items adorning the neck as a collar, *Papering the Body* shows an eclectic range of designs which experiment with the material and methods to create works that defy the perceived unwearability of paper.

Sea Flower. Rice paper, 2007. Evoking the magic of the underworld. By Violise Lunn.

Jum Nakao
Brazil

One tonne of paper, 700 working hours, 150 professionals: these numbers may hint at the backbreaking effort behind Brazilian designer Jum Nakao's collection of paper dresses, but the essence of the performance, titled *Sewing the Invisible*, which was staged at the Sao Paulo Fashion Week in 2004 can scarcely be measured in digits. Here's proof: the designer was deeply thanked by a cleaning lady who caught the performance by chance, "I think your work means: people are not important for what they carry outside, but inside."

The challenge of developing such an unconventional project – a collection of delicate and ephemeral paper dresses – had its thrills and spills. When Nakao's team first presented the nascent idea of a collection in paper to cellulose companies for funding, they were turned down. Eventually, they received support from publishing companies, and also Red Bull.

Then, there was the actual demands of developing the paper dresses themselves. One of the seamstresses on the team surprised herself by sewing paper. The make-up designers had to figure out how to recreate the look of a Playmobil fairy for the models. The right technology had to be applied to emboss and laser-cut the delicate dresses. And finally, the press department had to keep details of the show hush-hush: no one was to know the final twist – when the models would destroy the paper dresses on stage. Today, *Sewing the Invisible* is considered one of the most important fashions shows of the century by Musée Galliera, the fashion museum in Paris.

1 **Sewing the Invisible.** Vegetable paper, 2004. The paper reliefs were embossed by a traditional Brazilian engraving company; laser technology was used to cut the lacework of each piece. The vegetable paper gives the dresses a subtle transparency.

1

2

2 The scenographer designed anemone-shaped objects out of paper cones for the set; dressed in Playmobil wigs, the models appear like enchanting fairies on the catwalk.

3

3 Nakao takes inspiration from the forms found in the romantic era at the end of the 19th century; the dresses are delicate and light, suggestive of impermanence and the inevitability of loss.

4 Nakao applies volumetric constructions to the skirts and sleeves of the dresses, giving them a precious and romantic quality.

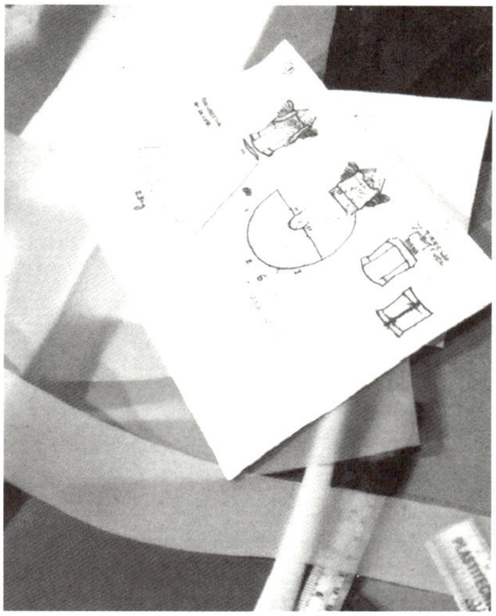

4

5

Why did you choose the material paper for your collection?
Paper is the realm of the sketch, of notes, and a part of the creative process [...] a white, unfinished, empty work, capable of becoming laden with meanings, with poetry, and with the lightness necessary for the work to flow.

Which period of fashion history did you reference for the garments?
For clothing I chose the late 19th century, a period where fashion was extremely elaborate and precious, both in volumes and textures. Those values would be crucial in causing in the spectator an instantaneous, intense feeling of wonder at the work.

What is the meaning of Sewing the Invisible?
We need to strip our souls bare to reveal our capacity to be light, to dream of the unsayable, the impossible, the inexplicable, the indefinable. And to associate the visible trace with the invisible, creating volumes, textures, colours, words, designs, openings and pathways toward a new thinking.
That is what it means to sew the invisible.

5 In the astonishing finale, the models tear up the paper skirts, corsets, sleeves and collars, delivering Nakao's poetic message: fashion is a medium and not an end in itself.

Papering
the Body

1

2

3

Giovanna Grimoldi

Italy

Madonna, Cindy Lauper, Loredana Bertè, Amanda Lear and Gigi Proietti have worn a dress by this designer: discovered by famous Italian fashion journalist, the eccentric Anna Piaggi, Giovanna Grimoldi's foray into the fashion world was propelled by a dress named the *Dress of Dolls* published in the review *Espresso* in 1988.

Grimoldi went on to design accessories, fashion sculptures and costumes for show business and design that have graced the pages of *Vogue*, *The Face*, *Moda* and *Donna*. In 1999, a series of Grimoldi's sculptural paper dresses were exhibited at the Louvre Museum, Paris, to celebrate the publication of *Doppie Pagine* by Piaggi, a book showcasing the classic "double-spread" pages by Piaggi as fashion editor of Italian *Vogue*. In 2007, Grimoldi also took part in an exhibition of sculptural paper clothes at London's Victoria and Albert Museum in *Fashionology*, an exhibition paying homage to Piaggi.

1 **Doppie Pagine**. Printed paper of different substances, 1999. A sculpture to be worn. The designer- made photocopies of fashion journalist Anna Piaggi's book *Doppie Pagine*, transforming the book into a piece of art.

2 **Cartiglio**. Cardboard of different substances painted to slope, 1999. A sculpture to be worn.

3 **Mare in Tempesta**. Paper cotton painted to slope, 1999.

Elisabeth Lecourt

France

Elisabeth Lecourt's first dress was a self-portrait: a paper dress expressing her thoughts back in 1997. Today, the French artist uses maps to represent the habitat and identity of the wearer. Her paper dresses are technically not fashion items, but the French artist folds and cuts these maps of cities into the familiar shapes of clothing. A series of buttoned-down dresses and shirts, pleated skirts and pressed sleeves are meant to be hung on the wall as works of art rather than actually worn.

2

1

3

1 **Une Souris Verte.** Map of World, 2006.
2 **Maman Les Petits Bateux.** Map of the United Kingdom, 2006
3 **Ne Pleure Pas Jeannette.** Map of the World, 2007.
4 **Ainsi Font Font Font.** Map of New York, 2006.
5 **Une Chanson Douce.** Map of London, 2008.
6 **Alouette, Gentille Alouette.** Map of London, 2008.

4

5

6

1

Michael Cepress
United States

At the invitation of Greek fashion curator Vassilis Zidianakis and Atopos, Washington-based designer Michael Cepress was given a vintage 1960s paper dress with a *Yellow Pages* print and asked to reinvent it into something his own. His artistic response took flight from a long-standing interest in historic menswear, classic tailoring combined with the challenge of creating compelling wearables with paper. "I'm deeply invested in the place where day-to-day wearables merge with art; where an ordinary garment becomes something more complex, more meaningful, more artistic or sculptural," says Cepress. Titled *Collars for the Modern Gentleman*, the small collection of collars for men was made in the spirit of historic paper collars from the early 1900s and was part of the exhibition *RRRIPP!! Paper Fashion*.

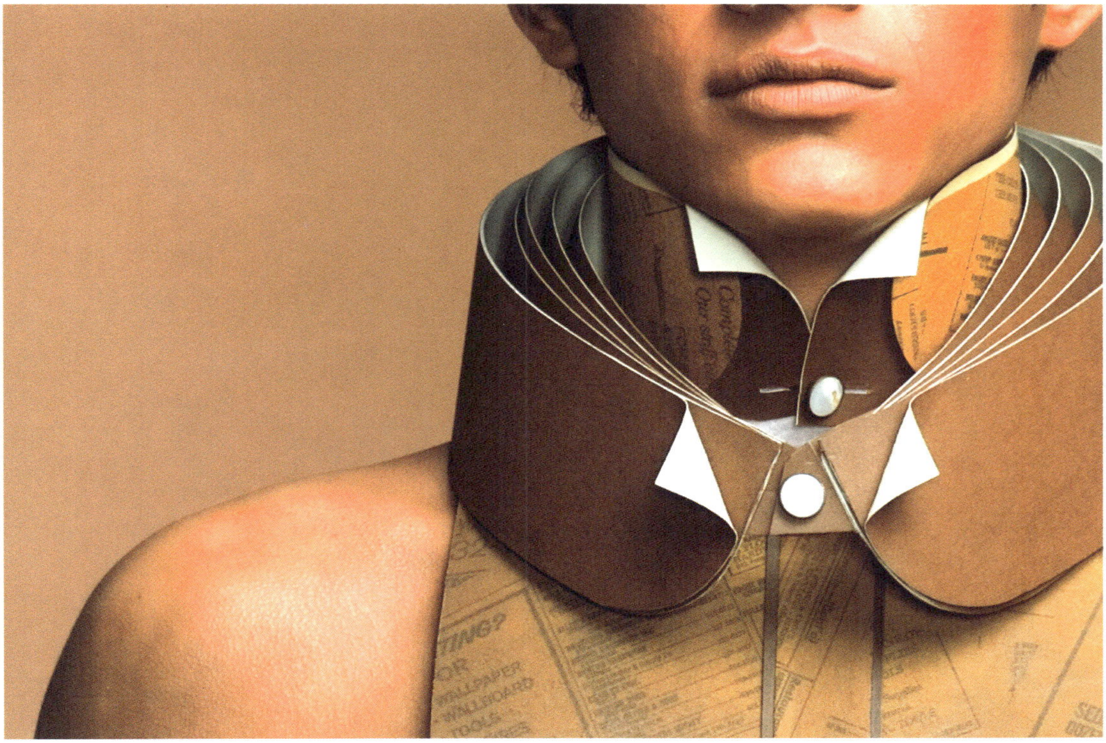

2

1–2 **Collars for the Modern Gentleman.** Vintage newspaper-printed Pop Art paper dress from the 1960s, found papers, spray enamel paint, ink and Edwardian collar studs, 2007.

3

When Greek fashion curator Vassilis Zidianakis approached you to remake a vintage paper dress, what was your response?
The piece offered me an interesting and challenging set of design problems to work with. Suddenly, I needed to work with paper in the same way I would otherwise work with fabric. It gave me a chance to take something historic – with a meaning and history of its own – and then change that into new work that somehow responded to its original state.

Is there a historical link between men's collars and the vintage dress you were working on?
I have long been fascinated with men's fashion at the turn of the 20th century. Tailored garments were highly fashionable at this time, and nearly all men wore detachable collars and cuffs affixed to their shirts. These collars were either made of paper or a stiffened fabric, and were sold rather cheaply. They were intended to be worn a few times, then discarded as they wore out, much like the paper dresses from the 1960s. The average person owned many of these collars, and could easily change the look and style of their dress very easily by simply changing the style of collar they wore.

Why did you choose to turn the dress into collars?
I find the structured, poised look of these collars to be incredibly beautiful, and wanted to do an iteration of them for this exhibition. With my designs, I wanted to keep the structured feel of the historic paper collars from the early 1900s, but also wanted to add more colour, texture and layering to the look of each piece. I wanted to reference the multiple layers of traditional men's clothing in each collar, so the lapel shapes you see come into play. It was my goal to give the sense of this layering effect often seen in men's clothing, but to also let it become more elaborate, more dramatic, and more sculptural.

What materials did you use to make the collars?
I found paper shirt fronts from the late 1800s that were also used in each piece as a base for the other shapes to attach. Each collar is closed with actual Edwardian-period mother-of-pearl and brass shirt and collar studs. These are the very same button or studs that would have been used with paper collars from that period.

3–4 **Collars for the Modern Gentleman.** Vintage newspaper-printed Pop Art paper dress from the 1960s, found papers, spray enamel paint, ink and Edwardian collar studs, 2007.

Licensed Electrical Contractors
24Hr EMERGENCY SERVICE
call 258-3789
night 271-9560
Restaurant & Cocktail Lounge
Imported & Domestic Wines

Martine Horstman

The Netherlands

Martine Horstman's paper objects can be interpreted as autonomous objects or as pieces of jewellery. The starting-point of Horstman's visual work is to make strong and movable constructions from paper, hence, her choice of Boomerang cards (cardboard), which have the right thickness for a strong construction. She cuts the cards and folds them into a harmonica shape. Colourful and rich in contrast, her objects form compelling ornamental forms on the human body.

1 **Spirally**. Boomerang cards (cardboard), 2002.
2 **Cyclical**. Boomerang cards (cardboard), 2001.

1

2

3

3 Cyclical. Boomerang cards (cardboard), 2001.

Polly Verity
Scotland

An artist based in Edinburgh, Polly Verity is avidly investigating the world of paper folding. In her experiments, sometimes an idea manifests through working with her hands, bringing her into an unknown path. "It is possible to break new ground with new types of folds," shares Verity, who has been investigating the possibilities of curved folds. She cites experiments with a scrap of paper which triggered a series of repeated curved patterns, "They looked like strange space construction pipes. This led on to further investigation and opened up many possibilities."

Verity's paper dresses are themselves a kind of visual spectacle. Geometrical patterns folded with razor precision on a clean white sheet produce striking forms; worn on the body, the human figure is changed into a sculptural piece of art, all lines, folds and shadows. Her paper dresses have been in fashion shows in Glasglow and Edinburgh, worn by the artist Anna Ellerington for her 2003 exhibition in New York, and even been commissioned for a wedding.

1

1 **Cyberchic**. Printer photo paper and cartridge paper, sticky-backed Velcro, polypropylene and hot glue, 2007-2008.

2 **Paper Dresses**. Printer photo paper and cartridge paper, sticky-backed Velcro, polypropylene and hot glue, 2007-2008. Geometrical pattern folds are pleat-packed into small solid bricks for ease of transportation and storage.

2

Tell us how your love affair with paper began.
In 1968, my grandfather, Eric de Maré wrote a book, *Your Book of Paper Folding*. This was a book with simple representational models. He inscribed a copy for me in 1979 which was immediately enthralling. I have been folding ever since. My designs have always been non-representational, abstract patterns. Sometime in 2006, I came across a small team of folders who posted their work to *Flickr*. This small community was very welcoming and I began to flourish under their encouragement and through collaborations with them. Suddenly, I was beginning to invent new folds which had to be the most exciting thing.

You seem to take your love of paper folding to an almost fanatical level.
I keep a sheet of paper by my bed in case I wake up in the night with an idea that I must try out before it's lost. When I'm out, I might try to "fold" the pattern of someone's geometric dress in my head.

Why do you only work with white paper?
White paper helps simplify the visual aesthetic of what is already a complicated structure. The shadows cast by the folded form can then be read without distraction and with maximum visual impact.

What kind of techniques do you apply to your paper work?
I mainly design the score patterns on a computer and then transcribe by slightly cutting or printing the lines onto paper. I score the lines over a light box with a not-to-sharp knife, fold along these lines, and then collapse the paper into its final shape.

What have you discovered about the process of working with paper?
Paper is a very challenging medium, strong in some senses but also very fragile. When I am working on a large scale, such as paper dresses, it can take two or three days just to fold the work and a slight tear, wrong crease or kink can ruin a piece of work, which could be a huge setback.

Are your paper dresses hard to wear? Is it easy for you to move around in them?
They are easy to wear, very light. As the wearer moves, the piece is animated; corrugations compress and open out and the movement of light and shadows are exquisite. The dresses are attached together with Velcro fastenings so as to ease the process of getting in and out.

How has the public responded to your paper work?
With incredulity mainly, especially when I explain that the dresses can only be worn once (the paper deteriorates very quickly upon wearing, especially with movement).

What are your feelings toward the paper works being produced today?
I'm thrilled by some of the work I see. I think the Internet has been extraordinary in connecting a few people with a particular fascination with paper to observe each others work, and really raise the quality and precision of work in this area.

3 **Paper Masks.** Printer photo paper and cartridge paper, sticky backed Velcro, polypropylene and hot glue, 2007-2008.

1

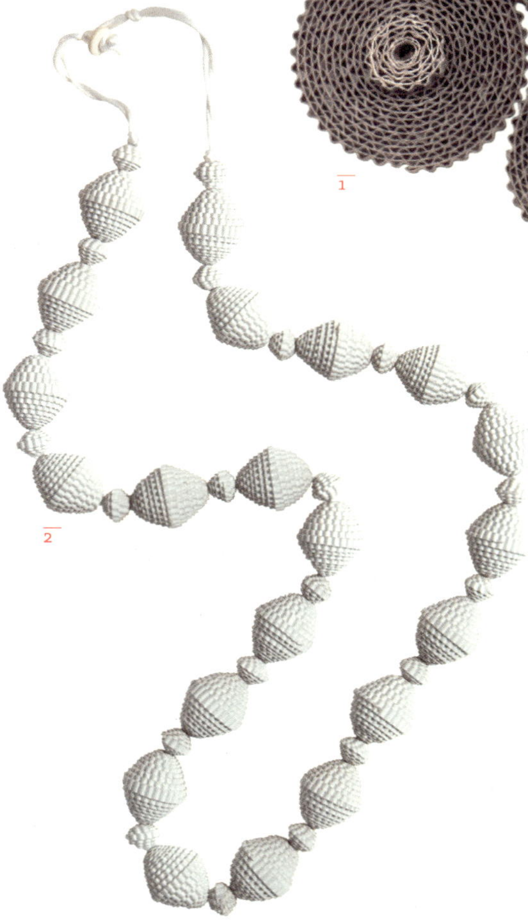

2

Angela Simone

Italy

"Working with glue, it is possible to obtain very robust beads that are also waterproof," explains jewellery designer Angela Simone, "My jewellery is not as short-lasting as some may think". While Simone's paper "jewels" may seem like precious items, the artist applies two techniques to make these paper items wearable: in the first technique, quilling, paper is rolled up to make them more sturdy and "hard-wearing"; in the second technique, marble paper (obtained from the Japanese *suminagashi* technique) is used on round, square or rectangular pendents. Simone works with a wide rangeof paper to create a variety of beads – big or small, broad or narrow, fat or slim, fussy or plain – combining them with other materials such as thread, cotton, hemp and gauze to create one-of-a-kind paper jewels.

1 **Together**. Corrugated cardboard, 2003.
2 **Prayer**. Corrugated cardboard, 2008.

1

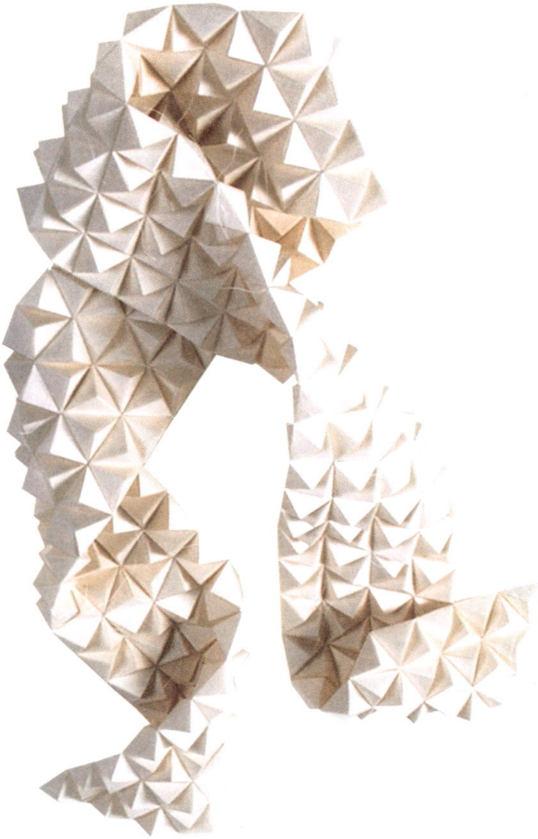

2

Zoe Keramea

Greece

Zoe Keramea's takes a strip a paper and folds it into a hexahedron, a geometric object with six flat sides and straight edges. The surfaces are knotted into themselves, forming a three-dimensional solid. Using the dipyramid as a module, Keramea builds new modular units. These are then sewn together into increasingly complex forms.

1 **Spiky Scarf**. Hand- folded and sewn paper hexahedra, 2007. A flexible sculpture that can be worn around the neck; commissioned for *RRRIPP!! Paper Fashion* by Atopos Cultural Organisation.

2 **Double Faced Unijewelery**. Hand folded and sewn printed paper hexahedra, 2006. These earring playfully reflect jewel facets.

Nel Linssen

The Netherlands

Dutch artist Nel Linssen has been asked much too often how long she takes to make a piece of paper jewellery. She started out in 1981 and has been making paper jewellery for several decades, producing numerous collections of bracelets and necklaces that are as elegant as they are attention-grabbing. These jewellery objects are the outcome of hours of direct experimentation, dedicated research and a sense of the artist's personal discovery.

As described in the artist's monograph, "Nel neither designs on paper nor devises her systems in advances... The minimalist logicality she eventually reaches is surprisingly enough based on a wholly intuitive process." There are no standard formulas for making these paper wearables. Her earliest pieces were made from strips of semi-gloss paper folded and threaded together to form a closed circle. Later collections of jewellery were put together without string, relying on a logical method of assembly to be constructed. She also started to plastic-coat the paper to allow herself to work more intensely with colour. In 1994, after attending a workshop where she worked with discs basked in clay, Linssen began to use the basic shape of the disc to give her jewellery an elegant, rotating construction.

Despite phases of experimentation with plastic and more baroque forms, Linssen has repeatedly returned to paper and to a discernable minimalist visual language. As one casts a retrospective glance on these collections of jewellery made in the 1980s and 1990s through to the millennium, the pieces still appear startling fresh. A subtle thread of continuity and coherence runs through the different collections, all bearing Linssen's careful, dedicated, intuitive signature.

2

1 **Bracelets paper/ Silicone cone tube.** 110gsm Elefantenhaut (Sanders Germany), 1996.

2 **Bracelets plastic coated paper.** 110gsm Elefantenhaut (Sanders Germany), 1989.

3 **Bracelets and necklaces.** Elefantenhaut 110gsm (Sanders Germany), reinforced kraft, Elefantenhaut stiffened with web of glass fibre, 1987-2002.

1

2

Violise Lunn

Denmark

There is something disconcerting about Violise Lunn's (un)wearable dresses: the sheer lightness and utter fragility of paper is crafted into objects which shimmer like apparitions. "I am often asked if it is not a bit schizophrenic to work both with paper sculptures and fashion," says the Danish fashion designer. These works resemble the shedded skin of a snake; the shoes twist like creeping insects; paper is crumpled, ripped, straightened, folded to create a desired appearance or ambience.

1 **Bleeding Heart**. Japanese paper, 2003. Finding beauty in the thought and image of rattling organs.

2 **Sea Flower**. Rice paper, 2007. Evoking the magic of the underworld.

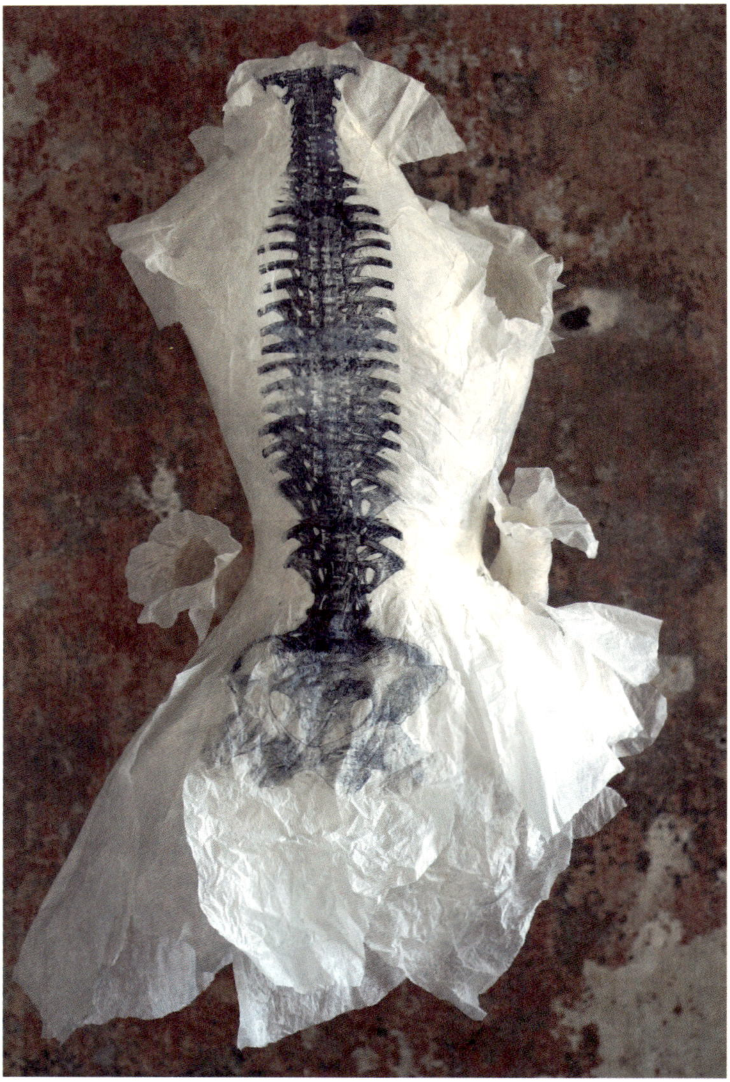

3

3 **Spine**. Pattern paper and print, 2003. The skeleton is out of the closet.
4 **Heart**. Pattern paper, 2003. This dress is as fragile as our insides.

4

What were some ideas which inspired your paper garments?
For one show, my inspiration was old prints of organs and skeletons. The result resembles dancing ghosts where one can almost hear the bones rattle.

What kind of treatment do you give the paper?
I treat the paper in many varying ways. I give the paper different surfaces with glue or paints or lacquer. I crumple, rip, straighten, fold.

What effect were you hoping to achieve?
The paper should look like a dream. I hope to give a feeling of something out of this world.

What do you feel about paper as a material?
Each type of paper is a material of its own right. Some are transparent, some are bulky, some are thick, others have colour or texture. The paper changes quality and structure in all kinds of ways depending on how I use it.

6

5 **Ballgown**. Pattern paper, 2007. An utterly useless party dress designed for the Denmark Biennale 2007.

6 **The Duchess of Luxembourg**. Newspaper, 2005. Swarovski stones are used on newspaper to create these shoes which look like antique currency notes.

Index

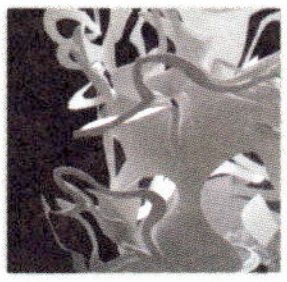

Jordy Yu Fu
www.jordyfu.com
p.98

Jum Nakao
www.jumnakao.com.br
p.154

Kako Ueda
www.kakoueda.com
www.georgeadamsgallery.com
p.10

Katie Kulper
www.katiemkuklper.com
p.134

Kylie Stillman
www.kyliestillman.com
p.64

Laura Cooperman
www.lauracooperman.com
p.30

Lizzie Buckmaster Dove
www.ngart.com.au/artists_buckmaster.html
p.62

Martine Horstman
www.martinehorstman.nl
p.170

Maslen & Mehra
www.voidgallery.com
p.136

Matt Gagnon Studio
www.mattstudio.com
p.108

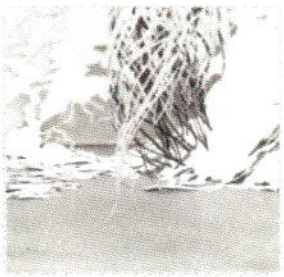

Mia Pearlman
www.miapearlman.com
p.128

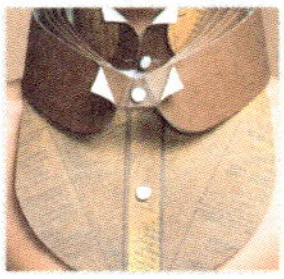

Michael Cepress
www.michaelcepress.com
www.atopos.gr
p.166

Miriam Londoño
www.miriamlondono.com
p.38

molo
http://molodesign.com
p.122

Nel Linssen
www.nellinssen.nl
p.180

Nendo
www.nendo.jp
p.116

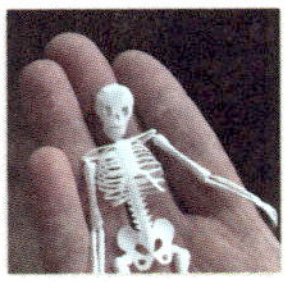

Peter Callesen
www.petercallesen.com
www.helenenyborg.com
p.46

Polly Verity
www.polyscene.com
p.174

Publique Living
www.publiqueliving.com
p.96

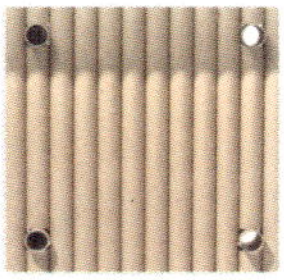

PUSH>
www.pushdesign.de
p.112

Robert Ryan
http://misterrob.co.uk
p.40

Schleeh Design
www.schleehdesign.com
p.78

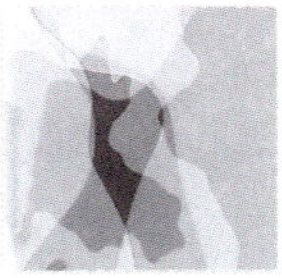

Shannon Rankin
http://selflesh.com
p.32

Sounds of Silence
http://soundsofsilence.de
p.146

Tokujin Yoshioka Design
www.tokujin.com
p.102

Violise Lunn
www.violise.dk
p.184

Zoe Keramea
www.zoekeramea.com
p.179

Acknowledgements

We would like to thank all the designers and artists featured for their kind permission to publish their works; all the photographers who have generously granted us permission to use their images; and Elaine Lee for the original idea of this book.